RAW, GIRTHY & CUT

BUSINESS SCHOOL FOR BASTARDOS

J. Bo Lawrence

First Edition

NEWMAN SPRINGS PUBLISHING
Meadville, PA

First originally published by Newman Springs Publishing 2025

Please note that the names and stories may or may not be as accurate as others' memories. Consider all characters fictional.

ISBN 979-8-89617-385-4 (Paperback)
ISBN 979-8-89617-386-1 (Digital)

Printed in the United States of America

I initially intended to have a finance- accounting professor or corporate finance bro audit the technical aspects of this book, but the editing process to publish, for text alone, is cumbersome enough! Plus, people are busy and nothing in life is free. I encourage all to audit my equations, formulas, and work. Do additional research on all topics mentioned in this book. Re-run my numbers in Excel. Errors happen in corporate finance and accounting every day. I have seen $20K purchases of dead inventory because of errors. I have seen controllers enter wrong debits and credits on journal entries that resulted in large errors on financial statements. In one instance, by discovering such an error, it led to me taking over as Director of Finance. Many on accounting teams don't understand how debits and credits impact all the various GL accounts. One of my mantras is to constantly audit. With that said, I may or may not have thrown in an intentional error or two for you to call out, buried in Excel formulas, accounting transactions, or business math word problems. If you find any, you are well on your way to becoming a B School Bastardo. The goal is to think, analyze, evolve, and have a better level of understanding in all areas of business. The devil is in the details; but for this book, principles matter most. And feel free to skim over the tables, charts, equations, and only read the words if that suits you. You'll get the most juice from that squeeze. This book was written when I was younger, maybe with a cruder sense of humor than I have now. But hey, I'm putting it out there and hope you will take it all in, light-heartedly. I have gravitated away from politics and more towards Christian faith & positive energy over the past years, in a pursuit to find peace. While I authored this book, most was written by a different version of me than I am now. May God bless your life and the universe surprise you with miracles. We need more love and positive energy in the world. – J. Bo

Introduction

I'VE STARTED THIS DAMN BOOK FOUR TIMES, and something always goes wrong. The first two times, I was a young tyke trying to write about my childhood and how it supports a conservative philosophy by demonstrating that people aren't beholden to terrible upbringings. In fact, if you were never molested and learned to be wary of creepy perverts, then your life wasn't all that bad (in my humble opinion). The problem with that book: It wasn't fun to go back and revisit a sometimes-shitty youth in detail. At times, it was tedious, and at others, emotionally intense. BTW, psychology is a crock of categorizations. I'm a numbers guy. For these reasons, it only culminated in a long-ass introduction slash chapter that never wanted to end.

When that book got put on hold, the only saved copy was in a personal email account used strictly for improprieties—a porn email, per se. Since those are now a thing of the past—as every major email and internet service provider willingly hands over all personal data to the NSA—many may be unaware of what I'm talking about. To hell with ya! Anyways, a girlfriend may have come into the picture. I may have been disgusted with my own moral integrity. Regardless, something happened, and I felt compelled to delete that account entirely—and the draft of my book with it.

Most recently, I shifted gears. An idea sparked about a book with a purpose that flowed like the wines of Santa Barbara County (my hometown region). I had an outline. I had a target audience. I got through an introduction and the first chapter. I was motivated to write every day. Then…fuck! I had my work saved on a flash drive, and that tiny piece of equipment disappeared. I was back to square one. God was testing the hell out of me. Did I have the motivation to start from scratch? Would whatever I cranked out be as good as the previous WIP's rhythmic flow I had developed? Should I throw in the towel on ever publishing a book and making money at writing altogether? Fuck money! This is about the truth. These confounding thoughts danced around in my head like a late night straggler on the dance floor, prowling for a late-night sex session.

Oh, hell nah! What kind of man folds like a deck of cards after a few setbacks? That would be the modern man—the man who believes everyone should win and no scores should be kept in sports. A man who believes his gender is fluid and has no God-given onus to protect the weak. That would be the man who believes people should not be held responsible for their actions. One who claims society is to be blamed at large when a crime is committed. As I follow that line of thinking, I think to myself, "So when some lowlife scumbag breaks into my house and steals my hard-earned cash money, we should throw handcuffs on the local community (me included) because we didn't give that jackass enough free shit in life?" Sorry, but that makes no sense to me.

These same simpletons will have you believe that college admittance and jobs should not be based on qualifications and experiences. To them, there is always some intangible factor to blame for the lack of success, namely race. To blanket everyone under race or ethnicity and a certain umbrella is racist in and of itself. There have been two historical arguments for affirmative action: (1) slave reparations to right past wrongs and (2) to ensure diversity in education or the workforce. Both pseudo claims need debunking.

Regarding "slave reparations," everyone's ancestors have been shat on at one time or another. Was slavery horrible? Hell, yes! Have Christians been enslaved? Have Jews been enslaved? Have Muslim women been enslaved? Yes, all these events happened over the course of history and were undoubtedly wrong. Have I shackled someone in my lifetime? Not unless for mutual sexual gratification. The

Emancipation Proclamation was over 160 years ago. Not sure if still there are many people who know a person who lived during that time. Here we are in 2025. Across the board and unanimously, nearly everyone reveres and celebrates the end of slavery in America. We all want equality regardless of race. Two wrongs don't make a right. Reversing discrimination just promotes hostility between races. It will never allow judgment to pass based solely on the content of character. If one racial group is getting additional help, then another isn't. For every individual admitted into a university (or job position), all things equal, with race as the determining factor, another person is left out in the cold due to the color of their skin. Society's obsession with past injustices will never allow progress and an honest path forward.

Combatting the nonsense behind argument number two for affirmative action requires color blindness. Diversity comes in many forms, not just racial and ethnic diversity. In fact, to say that all African Americans, Latinos, Asians, or Mixed-Anglos act the same is a racist mentality. If you are diversifying your student body or workforce based on race, then you assume every one of a certain race brings the same element of diversity to the workforce. That couldn't be further from the truth. I know people from all ethnicities who grew up in much nicer houses with a more stable family life than I ever enjoyed. I grew up with plenty of kids, whose parents (maybe) worked cash jobs (under the table), lived in bigger houses, and still got free lunches every day at high school. I was hustling to get by, coming from a broken, unstable Mixed-Anglo family (Czech, Scottish, Cherokee Native, English, etc., background). But white people have no ethnicity, right? We are just white crackers. Psyche! All people of the world have a beautiful, rich, mixed background to embrace.

I don't condone either of the lies that support affirmative action. However you spin it, the policy itself is a big bowl of malarkey and racism. Until every person is judged on the content of their character and actions (MLK Jr. style), we will never live in a world of true equality. There will always be excuses, bitter animosity, and people placed in positions based on color.

Like the majority of Americans, you weren't born into a well-connected family. Daddy and Mommy didn't have a million-dollar business waiting when you came of age. If you fucked up at a pivotal moment in life, no second chance. If grades were garbage in high school, a tall mountain to climb consisting of city college, state university, and lacking financial aid. Student loan debt and competing for underpaying jobs with bleak outlooks for future growth. This should be a wake-up call for young Millennials acting as entitled pussies for life.

Affirmative action and the omnipresent risk of failure aren't the only roadblocks preventing career success. The American dream is on life support, if not already dead. Society is chained by a sea of regulations and costly necessities deterring a happy, middle-class life. College costs an arm and a leg. If you are like me, your parents won't fund it, and you will come out of college with long-term debt that accumulates interest daily. Do you understand how much interest you pay over the lifetime of a loan? Are you apt at making financial decisions based on cash flow needs and capabilities? What is debt financing? How does it impact one's personal financial statements? One needs to manage their personal finances as a business.

What is your career path? Is that literature degree ready to secure big bucks upon graduation, or will you be stuck in purgatory as a teacher's assistant, living on a couch, and blaming society for not giving enough money to education? Growing up, we are constantly taught—brainwashed into thinking—one needs a job helping imaginary underprivileged people. In other words, one needs to be a social worker or teacher according to this philosophy. For a split second in time, I even considered it. "Wow, it would be cool to work with kids as a teacher and coach, making a difference." Truth is, if you want to work with kids that aren't your own, something may be wrong with you. When I think of the classic do-gooders of youth, Jerry Sandusky and the Catholic Church come to mind. They were all about "protecting" the children with a helping hand. Jerry Sandusky received awards from the Pennsylvania government for his work with inner-city youth, and the Catholic Church was a staple in little boys' lives all across the globe. How the hell did that go?

Having taught Brazilian Jiujitsu and coached youth football for many years, I have learned quite a bit about the coaching landscape. It is difficult to find good coaches who are out there for selfless reasons *(like giving back or teaching kids how to be good players & people)*, given the pay is nominal. All you have to do is follow the money. Since there is minimal money in coaching youth sports, you usually get stuck with people who are trying to promote their own kid's agenda, boost their own ego, or have a career in the education system & have the free time. Coaching can give educators an extra paycheck and the community clout of being a head coach. Since most corporate careers don't offer the flexibility of leaving early to coach practice at 4PM daily, the options are limited. For those coaches out there, who are doing a great job, nothing but love & respect. But for those that have ulterior motives, don't teach kids how to be good athletes & people, pick favorites based on money or politics, and generally do a poor job, what a shame. Kids deserve better. And for coaches who take advantage of their position of authority, zero tolerance there.

If you come from an elite ruling class, you might think this book isn't for you. That's hogwash. Steve Jobs was a bastard dad, and Bill Gates decided his posthumous wealth would be donated to charity, not his spoiled children. Growing up with kids who were set for life, I can still make the case that life lessons and financial aptitude can serve them especially well.

Now, I grew up hanging out with Mexicans whose families worked on ranches and wealthy football friends who had ranches themselves. I was always a true blue-collar type of kid. My parents divorced when I was four, and since then, I internalized most tragedies and handled things on my own. After getting an MBA and graduating Beta Gamma Sigma honors (GPA above 3.7 with a finance concentration) from Pepperdine while simultaneously advancing my corporate career in all things analytics, I was fortunate enough to work for one of the top equine supplement companies in the world, located in my hometown. This wasn't the usual crowd I associated with growing up in Santa Barbara County. I did have wealthy friends during my younger years, but the normal crew at my house for high school parties was also absent of parents. We were considered the bad kids. Even in fourth grade, Solvang Elementary School sent a notice home to our families that we had a "clique." A gang of mostly white and Latino kids, all with compatible personalities and a knack for mischief. No curfews. No rules.

If you are like me and grew up with no connections, you need to understand that you may lose out to someone because they have an inside track that you don't. We have all seen kids get into colleges, land high-paying jobs, and live a life due to who they know and not what they achieved. For that reason, you must be that much better than the other guy or gal who has the inside track. No nepotism means no paved future. You cannot simply be average and expect it to be good enough. You aren't an heir to any throne.

Now, if you are the heir to a fortune, the same rule applies for different reasons. Those born into wealthy empires will always be judged by their peers as having *been born* with a silver spoon in their mouths. Any successes or failures will be scrutinized, and the scarlet letter (*N* for *nepotism*) will always make others believe you did not earn something entirely on your own. People are obsessed with chatter, especially females. They talk about who is who, where they came from, why they are in the position they're in, etc.

Whether you have no connections or are born to the royal family, you must focus on competitive greatness and improving upon the plight you were given to succeed. Be a better person than your parents, in whatever way, shape, or form. Even if they founded a billion-dollar company, they may be pieces of shit as a father or mother. You can undo the wrongs that were done to you simply by being a good person to others. Then the talk will be about how nice of a person you ended up despite such austere (or auspicious) beginnings.

Then you have lunatics out there who claim to be "fairness police." Anything you do is considered greedy; although, them wanting to swoop in and eat up your paycheck (by way of increased taxes) is considered benevolent. What exactly is someone's "fair share" of contributing toward society? If you sat down with Milton Friedman, one of the most brilliant minds of all time on economic theory, he would make the case that free market capitalism is most efficient when people act in their own best interest. That means a free market exchange, without any interference, is the most fair and effective way for society to be run. It is difficult to argue against that self-evident truth, but people will cloud your judgment with sob stories of starving children and people who can't care for themselves. Cry me a river.

Let's look at the fairness police in California and how things function when crunching numbers. If you are a young tike in college or high school, maybe it hasn't hit you yet. You still believe the mumbo jumbo about government being the benevolent protector of the poor and disadvantaged. It's a lie. Nobody in Washington, DC, actually cares about you. They care about getting reelected, buying votes, and having bronze statues of themselves enshrined in history books forever and ever.

Here is how life actually works. Get used to it, unless you have the balls to do something about it. If you finish college and find a job, you will be lucky if a corporation pays you fifty thousand dollars per year for entry level. You will not be adding much value in the early stages of your career, regardless of what Mommy and Daddy tell you. You will be a plug-in cog who does a necessary job. At that job, the government is entitled to a certain amount of your pay. To put things into perspective, I dubbed Tuesdays "Fat Government Tuesdays" because 20 percent (one-fifth) of your paycheck goes straight to taxes or government entitlements, depending on your tax bracket. Think of it—an entire day of the five-day workweek is spent supporting the government. Do you feel one-fifth of your livelihood comes from the benevolent government? Absolutely not! If you follow the news, you can see just how much of that money is wasted on nonsense, vote purchasing, and redistributing wealth to the superrich while claiming it goes to the superpoor.

It only gets worse the more successful you become. Last time I checked, success should be rewarded, not punished. This isn't the case in the eyes of Big Brother Barack Obama, Crooked Hillary, Cigar Slingin' Bill Clinton, and the fairness police. When I reached the non entry-level point of my career and started adding significant value with complex quantitative analysis, I received a substantial pay increase,as shown below. My gross pay increased roughly 40 percent. Government taxes and bullshit increased ten percentage points. In essence, my net pay only increased 23 percent, while the government received a 110-percent pay increase. You can now factor medical costs into that government BS, as Obamacare offered anything but a free market choice. See below. The numbers are not exact (rounded), but the point is that you need to constantly be calculating where your money goes, starting with your gross pay.

	A.	*B.*	*C.*
	Start of career	Stage 2 of career	Expected percent increase
Annual Salary	$50,000	$70,000	40 percent

	Start of career	Stage 2 of career	Actual increase
Less: Government BS	20 percent	30 percent	10 percentage points
Government pay	$10,000	$21,000	110 percent
Your net pay	$ 40,000	$49,000	23 percent

The fairness police can go fuck themselves. Politicians, the same. Everyone wants to be all up in everyone's business when they can't even mind their own. We've got the NSA listening in on phone sex, checking out pervy email exchanges, and being the ultimate sex predators themselves. We've got Anthony Weiner's weiner uninhibited, yet he goes on tirades chastising everyone over greed and selfishness. Government money funds child molestation rings. Ask Jerry Sandusky and the state of Pennsylvania that supported his Second Mile charity with tax benefits and public support. Boy Scouts of America also has a great record for being a philanthropic, systematic pedophilia ring.

The United States of America is dead, but like a phoenix will rise from the ashes. Freedom lives in the backyard around campfires and minds of individuals who refuse to be sheeple of the masses. As I have climbed from the depths of a broken, dysfunctional family to top-tier Claremont Colleges to a corporate career in quantitative analysis to graduating Beta Gamma Sigma honors with an MBA in finance, I have learned invaluable life lessons along the way. There are certain inalienable and universal truths. I am not the same man today as I was when I graduated high school or college, nor will I continue to be stagnant at this stage of my life. The three guiding lights below have guided me as an analyst and logician to desired results alongside an incessant commitment to self-improvement:

1.) *Learning from past experiences and mistakes*—This means not only learning from your own but also being observant of others in your inner circle, the news, and characters both fictional and nonfictional. Insanity is repeating the same thing twice and expecting different outcomes.
2.) *Using numbers to paint pictures*—At the end of the day, two plus two equals four. No matter how many marketers try to convince you otherwise, math makes perfect sense of the seemingly complex. Dumbasses can add and subtract, but it takes intelligence to paint clear pictures from difficult concepts by applying number theory.
3.) *Common sense as a foundational pillar*—While math offers verifiable results, there are human factors involved in business and life. You cannot completely tune into one without considering the other. For example, a complex analysis may tell you something completely wrong if you cannot process extraneous factors influencing the numbers.

Sit back, strap on a jimmy, and throw out all the shit those indoctrinators from academia have taught you is real-world thinking. It's about to get real. It may turn raw, but who doesn't like it raw, ODB style? If I were to describe this book, it would be a mix of business tenets (à la *Rumsfeld's Rules*) for an Andrew Klavan young adult audience, with pragmatism & complexity of *Business Finance 101: What They Don't Teach in Universities,* topped off with the raunchiness of *I Hope They Serve Beer in Hell.* This, of course, is all to be done with my own personal narrative and style. Be original, if nothing else. That is my mantra. Enjoy!

Chapter 1

DOUCHE OF ELITIST FUNDRAISING

I GREW UP IN A SMALL TOWN IN Santa Barbara County that hosts some rich motherfuckers with ranches, real cowboys, surfers, and street kids. I hung out with a lot of the Mexicans whose families worked ranches or other labor jobs equally as the landowners themselves. We didn't care about your wealth; we cared about character. In a small town, you can't pretend to be something you ain't. If you pretend to be a tough guy, then prove it at a party in the riverbed and get in a scrap.

At Claremont Colleges, it was a culture shock. This was a top-tier, $45,000-plus-a-year university (now well over $60,000) that finished tops in college rankings year in and year out. Entering were some of the brightest, wealthiest kids in the nation. Average SAT scores at Claremont hovered over 1,450 (back when it was out of 1,600). That means you had to answer 90.625 percent of the questions correctly on the SAT test. I'm not sure if it is apples to apples, but to answer 90.625 percent correctly out of 2,400, you would score a 2,175. I'm sure they made it easier when they inflated the potential max score so everyone feels good and wins. But to give you an idea, a 1,340 SAT score puts you in the ninetieth percentile of test takers, meaning you scored better than 90 percent of the population. And yes, the average student at Claremont Colleges was better than that. I had a handful of college football teammates who scored a perfect 1,600 SAT score. In high school, you compete against people in your city and local surrounding areas in sports and academics. In college, that world gets bigger, going nationwide. Upon graduation, that competition goes global.

College was the first time being exposed to a world of elites—people who think they're better than everyone else because of socio-economic status. In my small hometown in Santa Barbara County, we had elites, but they hid it in every way possible. In pre-internet days, private wealth could be hidden. One couldn't Google someone's net worth and have an article in *Forbes* pop up. Those with ranches and millions in assets could blend in with the Mexicans and blue- and white-collar average Americans, so long as they didn't invite many people over to their house. And many of the wealthy did just that, maintaining more of a reclusive life rather than flaunting extravagance. Everyone wanted to be a member of the small community where high school sports were God.

In some ways, elites are better than everyone else (if you choose to be a superficial dunce that only cares about money and privilege). Not only that, but also in college and career, the system is gamed to cater to this crowd. Throw a few bucks into most social situations, guys and girls alike will drop their panties and give it up. In other words, elites have an easier path to success due to nepotism and special treatment.

Claremont Colleges had an interesting mix of elitists, arrogant academics, various ethnic groups, and athletes. I should have been a math major, but as an athlete who dedicated four hours to football almost daily during the season, I opted otherwise. Since I enjoyed a good party on Thursdays and weekends (plus a copious amount of weed), the math major thing would have cut into leisure time. Plus, I was still living under the impression that a career in accounting was incredibly boring, according to my mom, who hated my father's profession. Unfortunately, I really enjoy numbers and mathematics. Just because a career is boring to one doesn't mean it is for another. I would hate doing client services or social work, while some girls get all saucy from that stuff. But fuck it, to each his or her own!

I decided on the "study what I enjoyed most in the first year of college" route, which led me to an International Relations–History major. While I may have strayed from the natural and most profitable post-collegiate path of being a mathematician, I did harness critical writing skills into what they are today, which has served my career in many ways. I gained global exposure by studying abroad in Chile. I was at the cutting edge in an understanding of economics across a newly globalized world economy. From corporate communication to articulating political opinion in published pieces, Claremont prepared me extremely well. It truly was a world class experience. Every graduate that left Claremont was at the forefront of their peer group in terms of being able to excel, analyze, have an unrivaled knowledge base, be prepared to go above & beyond, and outcompete those who attended lesser universities.

The Claremont Colleges even planted the seeds for pursuing action in politics, culminating in a valiant run for local office. While I didn't win, it was a great experience that resulted in 2,700-plus votes, the endorsement from the biggest local paper, and lifelong access to the local political scene. I fondly look back on my twenty-six-year-old self with pride as that "young kid who was the Trump before Trump." My campaign was fearless and we battled head to head against Obamacare, police force corruption, and every government swamp that existed across the board. It is ironic that the Santa Barbara News-Press was the only newspaper publication to endorse President Donald J. Trump during his 2016 campaign and endorse the youngest-ever local city council candidate—me. One never knows how different experiences will blossom, and they are usually in ways unexpected.

Regardless of how you feel about Trump, our campaign predated him and the audacity was similar. I respected the "zero fucks" mentality of his early years when he was battling very real internal government corruption. When he started promoting big pharma and the vaccines, something changed in my opinion. I don't believe we should bomb & murder Venezuelan boats (people) delivering the most pure form (least dangerous) cocaine to America when the alternative is fentanly from China. The older I get, the more I can't stand politics or almost any politicians. It is difficult to follow anymore and I truly miss the days when politics was an academic topic more so than a social media firehose frenzy.

I arrived in college with a long-distance girlfriend. Bad call. I also arrived in college expecting there to be hot, collegiate women everywhere looking to party. False optimism, being at a nerd school. Claremont had a few hidden jewels in terms of girls, but the social scene wasn't catered to meathead animals from small towns that enjoyed fighting for women rather than touting esoteric knowledge on the Roman Empire to get their peckers wet.

On the first weekend of partying at Claremont, a few friends visited from my hometown. While out, we ran into a group of Pomona College elitists, and one of the girls had an eye for us. She gave us a slutty look, so we began chatting her up. The scene started getting rowdy, and we were all crushing beers. One of the biggest idiots in their crew had been talking in a fake British accent the entire time, claiming to be the lead singer from Radiohead. What an idiot, right? We thought so too, but this was probably the type of guy who still managed to get laid in a private university setting. To make a long story short, his act went on for long enough, and he started talking shit. I wasn't having it, so I form-tackled him, slammed him to the ground, and gave him a solid punch in the face that left him collapsed on his back with blood splurging from his nose. We bailed, and that was that. Big ol' campus security wasn't quick enough on that golf cart for us to have an encounter, but they would have gotten the smoke too. Street smarts lesson number one: never encounter authorities and never talk. Always bail before police or anyone else who can arrest you arrive.

The point of my first weekend is the fact I was a black sheep at Claremont. Santa Barbara County fighting customs and manhood were thrown out the window. There was a large gap between my definition of cool at the time and the elite, academic definition of cool. Lost in this sea of pretentiousness, I found a lifeboat in the form of a roommate of the same breed. His name was Randino Dingling, a.k.a. the Legend. He essentially gave the nickname to himself, which most greats do, by wearing a faded black T-shirt with the phrase "THE MAN" and an arrow pointing up and "THE LEGEND" with an arrow pointing down in bold, white block letters. His favorite swaggy outfit included a pair of jean shorts, high-top boots, and a sleeveless flannel shirt he cut himself a la Bill Belichick. Randino was the gentle, three-hundred-pound defensive lineman who had fought campus security along with other legendary drunken tirades that struck fear in the heart of Claremont's dean of students. Randino was one of the kindest, most stand-up guys one would ever meet. Behind that Bic razor-shaved head and Viking goatee, he was a total softy. But he did enjoy playing up the savage persona, and sometimes it did come out after slamming a twelve-pack or two.

While other students found solace joining nerd groups or student clubs, Randino and I preferred getting super baked off schwag weed and watching Korn videos in a black-lit room or playing quarters with the hippie chicks from down the hall. We were outcasts. What else could we do at an elite, private school? We'd buy an ounce of weed so cheap it ripped like cardboard and play video games. We would time how fast we could beat the original *Mario Brothers* on Nintendo and have all-night epic battles playing multiplayer *Halo* against our dormmates over a LAN network on the original Xbox console.

Outside of sports, video games, and playing Beirut, football players were not the favored group at an elite academic university. It was frowned upon by liberal professors and students alike to display any signs of testosterone or to present antithesis arguments against a pro-government agenda. There are ample examples I could give from this world of academia of the discrimination Randino and I encountered for being small-town white brutes with working-class parents. None stands out more from freshman year (and all four years) than one that involved Claremont's director of fundraising. This was the guy that went around befriending the student body during their time on campus so that when they graduated, he would have a relationship in place to ask for alumni donations.

The Douche of Elitist Fundraising was the boat-club type. He wore Dockers, penny loafers, and wire-rimmed glasses. He could be found lingering around the dorms or frequenting sporting events. Some people perv around on hot chicks. Others try to kick it with the cool kids. Some students got their rocks off kissing professors' asses. The Douche of Elitist Fundraising was a whore for Claremont's elites or those he had decided were destined for wealth.

His job was to cozy up with students until, at one point, he had them cornered in a dark room or at some awkward moment to ask them for a donation. Who knows? Maybe he'd offer up a rim job in exchange. I didn't know how the proposal went as Randino and I were invisible to the D of Elitist Fundraising. From my perspective, the scene had a very Scientologist feel to it. It seemed concocted. The Douche of Elitist Fundraising acted like Randino and I were non-students at Claremont. He would come to our dorms, talk with some of the other football players, but never introduce himself or grace us with his presence. The only time he did talk to us was when he dropped by one time and asked for another student who lived in our dorm suite.

If you look quantitatively at the Douche of Elitist Fundraising's tactics, one could guesstimate he was catering to the top 10 percent of students in terms of their parents' wealth. If your parents were millionaires, he would surely introduce himself and start deploying Scientologist tactics. He may have even offered personality tests and backdoor hand jobs for top-tier elites. John Travolta and Tom Cruise would surely do the same to acquire a new member of the church.

Claremont had roughly 1,200 students. The Douche of Elitist Fundraising catered to roughly the top 10 percent of Claremont's student population. If he was able to achieve ten times the donation amount per student by targeting the elites rather than the entire student body, including folks like Randino and myself, he would still be missing out on significant future donations.

The strategy employed by Mr. D was fatally flawed for many reasons. First, looking strictly at expected numbers shows that if you can get the bottom 90 percent of students to average $100 each in annual donations upon graduation, that group is valued at $108,000 annually. That is a very low expectation and easily achievable. In contrast, let's say you got the top 10 percent (ninetieth percentile—meaning their family's income was better than 90 percent of other students at Claremont) to donate ten times what the rest of the student body donated annually. You get these 120 elite students to average $1,000 in annual donations. That annual value is $120,000. Being the Douche of Elitist Fundraising, you think your strategy is robust. You target one-tenth of the student body, get an annual donation value of $120,000 versus $108,000 (from the other 90 percent), and still come out $12,000 ahead by doing 10 percent of the work. This portrays the Douche of Elitist Fundraising's archaic worldview at Claremont Colleges. He was banking on a few big fish to donate while neglecting a vast majority of the Claremont student body population, especially folks like Randino the Legend and myself.

Never go into an analysis with preconceived notions. Have a theory or hypothesis based on historical experience, but never assume that will play out in any given study. The D of Elitist Fundraising seemed amateur in his career now that I look back. Maybe he was raised to only rub elbows with the big-money people at the time. At Claremont, everyone had the potential to go off and have successful careers given their test scores and the top-tier education they were in the process of achieving. The tactic of targeting the Claremont students with wealthy parents was very near-sighted. At the time, it never felt right. I felt disrespected. The Legend felt disrespected. But how did it all play out? Putting things into a table clarifies. That is the difference between an analyst and a salesman. A salesman will talk through this entire scenario as I just did above. To truly analyze, you need to have a simple visual of what is going on.

	Formula	# of Students	Avg. Annual Donation	Annual Value
Top 10 percent of Student Body	= 0.10 × 1200	120	1,000	$120,000.00
90 percent of Student Body	= 0.90 × 1200	1,080	100	$108,000.00
Claremont Totals		1,200		$228,000.00

The elite fundraising expert simply needed to put the table above onto paper to realize that his approach to only developing relationships with the ninetieth percentile missed out on a group that was not much lower in value, given some assumed numbers. Furthermore, he had no idea how each student's career would develop post-Claremont. Ironically, some of the most successful Claremont alumni weren't the ones who were revered for having rich parents while in college. Speaking of douches, one of my favorite teammates, a hard-hitting safety named Cristoffer Duvalini, ended up being the founder of all these subscription services that deliver rad retro or fan goods to your doorstep on a monthly basis. In 2016, their revenues exceeded $100 million, and they raised an additional $18.5 million to fund expansionary ventures. Bottom line, my college football teammate founded and runs a $100-million-a-year company. He can be seen on the covers of different tech and business publications.

The funny thing about Duvalini is that he came into Claremont as the epitome of a douchebag and earned the nickname "Douchebag Duvalini" from our core football group. He was one of those guys always talking shit sarcastically, and you couldn't tell by his demeanor if he had the world's smallest dick or the world's biggest. I care not to speculate, but that was his style and attitude. We used to all banter back and forth, but Duvalini got the most trash talked to him because he was always talking a ton of shit. Not only did he turn out to be a hard-hitting, stud football player (whom I loved roaming the defensive backfield with, looking to lay hits), but he also transformed his *douchiness* into becoming one of the coolest kids at Claremont, all while embracing his persona. I love the guy. And the guy could probably make a hundred-thousand-dollar donation to Claremont and not even think about it.

With his semi-celebrity status, Duvalini has come across as humble and more mature since his days at Claremont. I'd never tell him that to his face, though. Don't want to boost his ego even more. But I guarantee the real douche, the Douche of Elitist Fundraising, never gave Cristoffer Duvalini the time of day during his time at Claremont because he was just a football player from San Jose with average income-earning parents, it seemed.

And on the flip side, I do glance at the Claremont Alumni Magazine to see who donates year in and year out. I almost never see some of those who were targeted during their time at Claremont for having elite parents. Yeah, there have been a select few, like Sarah Bambino, whose dad donated millions to build a huge cultural, academic, and sports complex, but she is the only one that comes to mind. Absent are those who walked around with elite arrogance because Daddy had them a job lined up to carry on the family business. People like myself and Randino the Legend, who came from nothing, are the types that take pride in having the ability to give back. That makes us feel like we have achieved. And despite the Douche of Elitist Fundraising's neglect, I have made donations to Claremont over the years. Nothing huge. Nothing consistent, as the politics of the current president annoy me, but had the Douche of Elitist Fundraising given me the time of day, my donations would be more frequent and more valuable.

This simple example from college may seem like I'm a bit butthurt. But replace the above story with how you flirt with and treat chicks from high school. You may think focusing your game with the ninetieth percentile, in terms of hotness, is a great approach. But your analysis is flawed because your shortsightedness doesn't account for hot girls that get fat and ugly chicks that get hot in the post-academic years. I've seen it happen both ways. Trust me. Let's make some key points one should consider when delving into any quantitative analysis:

1. *Never assume.* Analyze assumptions. Pull historical data on assumptions—You know what they say about assumptions? They make an ass of you and me (ass + u + me = assume). The Douche of Elitist Fundraising assumed his time was best spent going after the big fish. Some rich people are rich for a reason, in that they aren't always generous. If Mr. D of Elitist Fundraising had experience working with students who went on to have great success stories, he would have changed his assumptions and tactics for garnering the most valuable total donations at Claremont. He would

have targeted everyone the same. He would have blown up his model and realized that hot girls get fat and ugly girls get hot once they discover yoga and how to take care of themselves.

2. *Scrub, audit, rinse, repeat*—One will never put forth a quality analysis if it is grounded in bad data. First and foremost, one needs to audit all data for accuracy. If you can pull data from multiple sources and cross-verify, great, do it. If you have historically verified analysis with linking measurements, cross-check that shit. For example, if you are pulling donation history for a given date range and the average donation value is $10,000 when you know historically it has been in the $100 range, you know there is a problem. Dig in deep. Girls usually don't like small wang energy. And nobody likes a shallow, surface-scratcher analysis.
3. *Test and retest assumptions*—It is paramount going into any quantitative analysis to be confident of your assumptions. It is key to test a range for each assumption using extreme max and min scenarios to see how totals could change. From the example above, we have a constant (number of students) and two variable assumptions (donation per alumnus and success rate). We input speculation as to the Douche of Elitist Fundraising's perspective on two different target groups based on his interactions with the student body.

Constant	Assumption	Assumption	Variable Calculation
Number of students	Donation Per X	Success Rate =	Total Group Alumni Donations

Ask yourself, what are the max and min amounts for donation per alumnus and success rates that one could see for each group? How much does that change the analysis? What is the expected range of outcomes? Substituting in a 25 percent success rate and multiplying the donation per alumnus by ten yields much stronger results.

Maximum Scenario

	Constant	*Assumption*	*Assumption*	*Variable Calculation*
	Number of Students	Donation Per X	Success Rate =	Group Alumni Donations
Top 10 percent of student body	120	*$10,000*	*25* percent	$300,000
90 percent of student body	1,080	*$1,000*	*25* percent	$270,000
	1,200			$570,000

The maximum scenario above shifted the annual donations total from $228,000 to $570,000 (with donation per student increased and success rates added). This demonstrates why assumptions for any analysis must be realistic and tested for extremes. Anyone who presented Annual Douche's analysis as truth would look like a complete moron when assumptions deviate from what was originally expected.

4. *Acknowledge and deal with outliers (or don't)*— The real world is full of outliers. Think of a bell curve with a normal distribution of the population. There will be extremes on both sides and then a cluster in the middle. For example, most people will score average on a test, and then you have some people who totally bomb and others who ace the damn thing. Relating to the analysis above, Douche of Elitist Fundraising excluded outliers from his initial assumptions completely. He did not consider that there could have been an outlier in the 90 percent of the student body group with working-class parents who went on to become a multi-billionaire and would have bought Claremont a new campus had they been targeted and treated with equal respect from the get-go. If you dwell in a world of averages, you may be hit with unexpected anomalies that make you appear to lack foresight. Be aware of extreme cases from both sides and their impact. Mr. Douche not only lost out on significant donation amounts from the 90 percent of the student

body group, but he could have missed out on an unexpected gold mine if one of those kids went on to become the next Bill Gates or Steve Jobs. Cristoffer Duvalini is a great example of that.

5. *When possible, use historical data*— Maybe the Douche of Elitist Fundraising had verifiable, quantitative data that showed exactly his historical success by income level for past campaigns. I would bet my britches that he didn't. His tactics were pedestrian and demonstrated an approach grounded in elitism, not verifiable data. Anyone with half a brain knows Claremont is full of students who will be successful after college and willing to give back to their alma mater that helped them achieve success. It could easily be demonstrated if one ran an analysis on historical donations by parents' income levels. I guarantee it would be across the board and surprising who donated the most and who would be more likely to donate. However, any time historical data can be used for an analysis, it's a good starting point. If there are significant deviations, you don't explain them with, "Well, I thought this and decided to use these numbers for my assumption." It is a much better defense to say, "Historically, this is how we performed, which was used for the analysis, but we deviated because of these factors." For example, you may be able to increase the success rate on annual donations by solid percentage points and deviate from historical performance by simply targeting the entire student body instead of only the top 10 percent as Douche of Elitist Fundraising had been doing prior. Historical actuals are the best starting point for analysis, even if the plan is to deviate and improve. But use historical to put together a forecast, always.

6. *Be honest in regard to known unknowns*— Having worked under the scrutiny of many micromanagers and high-maintenance prima donnas, I have come to realize that some people question just for the sake of questioning. They

may have zero knowledge of how difficult the analysis is you just put forth, nor would they be able to achieve 10 percent of the same level of complexity if they attempted your job, but they will challenge any analysis to feel they added value. This should be expected and embraced. For example, in the original speculation about how Mr. Elitist Fundraising was targeting the Claremont student population, we had little to no information other than viewing his actions around campus. Essentially, there were only two knowns: (1) he was discriminant in his treatment of students in some way, and (2) there were roughly 1,200 students on campus. From that, we were able to put forth a set of assumptions and make a pretty strong case for what was going through his mind as he poached around dorm rooms hunting for future donors. If we are to be completely honest, the analysis is quite weak and based almost entirely on speculation. That is the simultaneous power and danger of numbers. If you put out an analysis and paint it as fact, if it proves to be wrong, you can lose credibility. That is why it is important to always acknowledge the shortcomings and factors that are unknown to any analysis. These can be footnotes that only the truly astute will read, but put them in there to cover your ass every time.

7. *Include notes at every step of process (can be fine print)*—Trust me, as a quantitative analyst, people will be wary, insecure, and frightened by the fact that you speak to numbers and not feelings or emotions. Most people want to have discussions in the world of "I feel," "I think," and "I know" without having anything to base their assumptions on. If you go into a meeting with the hard data to back up what you are saying, the simpletons will peacock up and try to find holes in your analysis. Despite the fact they would have no clue where to begin an analysis on the level you just performed, they will have diarrhea of the mouth and attack you from all angles. It is important to combat or

minimize this by including fine print notes that support and explain how and why your logic led you to the results it did. Some know-it-all is out there just waiting to stump you with a, "Well, what about this or that or this or that, blah, blah, blah." Give them the shit sandwich. Start with, "That's a great point! I took that into account like this..." Then you go on to either explain or let them know you are more than willing to delve deeper into the point they brought up. It makes them feel important and you seem like you are subservient to them as a good little data boy or girl. Even better is when you make them look like the clown asses they are, stating, "Well, that was addressed in the notes that explain how that group was handled or why a certain segment was treated in a certain way." Basically, put it all out there. Most times, people are operating at a much lower level and do not understand heavy analysis. If you include the details, it only gives your work additional support and credibility. It will also leave less wiggle room for those peacock women to make ignorant comments because they fear numbers more than death.

8. *Analyze nonquantitative factors*— Every quantitative analysis brings with it a special set of nonquantitative considerations. They may be ethical, political, sociological, philosophical, or commonsensical. For the Douche of Elitist Fundraising to treat people disparately due to socioeconomic status really made me feel like that guy was a piece of shit. Others may say he was just doing his job. That is an ethical dilemma. Ethics are an omnipresent, unresolvable factor because they pin two ideas of right against one another. My ethical code states that treating people differently because of who their mommy and daddy are is wrong. Some rich shmucks may believe Douche of Elitist Fundraising was best utilizing his time to achieve the objective of his job. This is a very common nonquantitative consideration—the human factor. You may be asked to analyze

numbers on the performance of certain peers against one another. Some peers may be outperforming others, but you need to bring nonquantitative considerations into the analysis if the numbers don't speak fairly. For example, Ms. Mujer may have a difficult time closing sales on the phone, but she makes up for it in other ways, being the first one in the office, the last one to leave, and the one who performs tedious tasks that other workers refuse to do. As an analyst, you must analyze the full picture, which includes nonquantitative factors.

9. *Revisit analysis to ensure results don't change over time*— B students will finish their analysis and never look back. Sometimes an impatient manager will push you to complete an analysis before enough time has passed for results to normalize. This is often the case, which is why it is important to never file away an analysis and never look back, especially with customer segmentation and marketing analysis, where a short-term gain may not mean long-term results. A professional analyst must be both near- and far-sighted. If you give a customer group a promo to increase their ordering frequency, it may show a short-term spike in sales that came in sooner than expected but may lead to a long period where they don't purchase. So your company basically threw a promotion at them for no reason. Constantly monitor, adjust, and refine any analysis. Keep your thumb on that pulse.

10. *No room for affirmative action in bell curves and/or life*— I'm going to reference the Douche of Elitist Fundraising one more time to blast a hole in his flawed approach once again. The guy had an affirmative action loophole to his strategy of going after future donors. Believe it or not, there was one student he would approach who didn't come from a wealthy family, nor display anything spectacular in terms of personality, athleticism, or academic abilities. Yes, he

targeted a friend of ours, who lived in the same dorm suite with us, for the fact that he was African American. The irony here was that my friend, whose name I will reserve, was not only from a non-elite family, but he was also having academic and other issues at Claremont. He wasn't on a path to graduate as he had neglected taking Spanish. He ended up scheming a way to test for his requirements, but there were some sketchy things the entire time, and he did not fit the bill for Mr. Douche of Elitist Fundraising's target group. But Douche of Giving would come by, act like he didn't know Randino the Legend or me, and ask for our African American teammate/suitemate. He would have life talks with him and treat him like he was destined to be the next Rockefeller once he graduated. This made the rest of us feel like outcasts, as if we weren't in the select circle of Claremont elites. The story ends up that our suitemate never had a consistent career after college. He may now; I don't know. And I always liked the guy and considered him a friend. But his career path can be described by the fact that he showed up at another one of our suitemates' and his Claremont wife's home, lived in the bottom of their three-story house for years, never paid rent, and never worked. Eventually, our other Claremont friend and his wife got tired of the basement dweller bringing home random Tinder dates, and they both parted ways. I hope that our former suitemate is doing well now, and he is a very bright, cool guy. He was definitely smarter & more successful than many of the college kids being targeted for fundraising efforts based on their family wealth. Again, race needs to be take out from how you view someone. It simply isn't right. Never let affirmative action, race, politics, or ethnicity skew any analysis or predetermine a desired outcome. You'll end up as a bottom feeder dwelling in basements.

Life and analysis are boxes of chocolates. Things rarely turn out the way you expected them to go in. That isn't to say the results surprise your rational mind, but one always learns something along the way when being unbiased and open-minded in analytics. That is the beauty in business analysis. You are in charge of the picture that gets painted. You can speak to the numbers while analyzing external factors not told by the numbers. The level of insight and foresight is what differentiates a data reporter from a true data analyst. The power is all yours. Use it wisely and do not be manipulative.

Claremont's fundraising money slave, the D of Elitist Fundraising, took an approach to fundraising that brought up serious issues for how to go about proper analysis. For the men, I hope someone told you to be nice to all the girls because, down the road, one of those fat, ugly chicks with thick glasses may blossom into a beautiful butterfly. For girls, you were probably told to be nice to acne-faced nerds because one day they may blossom into successful entrepreneurs with stapled stomachs turned six-packs. Look at the transformations of Zuckerberg and Bezos respectively. Like what?

The same lesson can be learned from the Douche of Claremont. It is ethical to treat people with an equal level of respect regardless of job title, looks, socioeconomic status, race, etc. Much like you never know which caterpillar from high school will end up the lovely butterfly, you never know the value someone will bring to your life until much later. Every interaction should be viewed as planting a seed. If you plant bad seeds, you may end up with a *Little Shop of Horrors* monster that comes back to bite you in the ass. If you nurture every seed with respect and care, you never know which will turn up and help you at some point down the road. Who knows, you may even get laid by the newly transformed hot chick if you act right.

Chapter 2

CARTOON CARICATURE EMPLOYEES

Go back to elementary school. Put yourself in that classroom with snot-nosed kids sporting messy hair and dirty clothes. How would you describe these menacing puke faces? Everyone had a personality. Everyone had a distinct look. Was everyone the same? No, but each was memorable in his or her own way, right?

The corporate world brings about a lot of similarities to schoolyard dynamics. People develop insecurities at a very young age. People don't change much, and one cannot completely detach from earlier years. The main difference between the kindergarten classroom and the corporate setting is that many people develop another layer of personality and compound complexes, adding on to childhood persona. Some reinvent themselves and mask elementary school insecurities with even more bothersome personality traits in the workforce.

There is that "smartest person in the room" who scraped by in high school and still barely reads or writes. He or she will come to work every day and preach about what kind of food everyone needs to eat, even when the mirror reflects a 250-pound behemoth of a human. They bring with them a heightened level of hysteria mixed with falsified omniscience. When they motor off at the mouth, you can't tell at any given second if they're going to break down and cry or shout down the entire room in a fit of rage. Bitchy. Entitled. Ugly inside and out. They treat others like slaves. They have terrible ideas, but you listen because nepotism or affirmative action put them in a position above you. Their mommy or daddy may own the company. They blame you for their mistakes. They throw you under the bus. They are out to get you. They will make you want to walk out on the job, go home, and never come to work again. They are your peers. This is one example of a personality type that covers the workforce like duck butter on lower backs in the swampy heat of a Louisiana summer.

The corporate office is a place where you go and hang out with people, many of whom you dislike, for at least eight hours on weekdays for the rest of your life. You cannot avoid it. You can change companies, but there will always be the next annoying person and their atrocious office habits. Corporate culture is distinct at every company. Each company has positives and negatives. Two of the most important factors that should impact a decision of whether to take a job are:

1. *Job* location—I lived in no man's land Nevada for my first job. While it was necessary to get the first job experience, I never should have lived in the biggest shithole in America with nothing to do for locals besides drink and go to brothels. Granted, it has changed from the John Wayne days when I lived there, but it will never have year-round warm climate or beaches.
2. *Corporate culture*—There are annoying people at every company, but corporate culture is all-encompassing. It mends people to act toward a given style that is acceptable at the company. The owner may even encourage the hiring of specific types that "fit the mold." If that mold happens to be condescending arrogance, you are fucked. If it is an environment where an active lifestyle and work-play balance is respected, a shitty job is more bearable.

As you progress through a corporate career, you will undoubtedly encounter some real pieces of work, both good and bad ones. You will also encounter some consummate professionals who are able to put their bad habits into remission for eight hours a day, show up to work, and treat people with respect. The spectrum is broad, but below are a few of the memorable cartoon character employees from my corporate career. Start thinking of how you would like to be portrayed when your peers have a few beers and talk shit. Think of how your cartoon caricature employee would look if you were painted in this book. Here is a list of how I would describe some:

1. *Absentee manager*—He "barelyyy" comes into the office. Nobody knows where he is, but they have a pretty good idea. They have seen him sitting at home, hanging out with his bratty kid, and doing house chores while everyone else is in the office doing dreadful work to make the world go 'round. His workweek is spent on leisurely activities. He can be found driving a lifted truck, running errands, working on his bronze, or playing wiener tag while his wife is out having an affair. One thing is for certain, the guy hardly works, and every employee knows it. However, he comes into the office once a week pumped-up, full of arrogance and demands, making anyone who crosses his path feel like a pee-on. He can maintain his position as BOSS (big old sack of shit) man because nobody is above him in that office. His daddy got him to skip middle management and thrust into a CEO role despite a lack of legitimate qualifications. He only answers to a parent company in a faraway land, at which he succeeds, since he is a great schmoozer and user on the phone. Fortunately, hell hosts a lovely place in the afterlife for the absentee manager. He will be forced to sit in the office all day long, chained to a non-ergonomic chair, wearing tighty-whitey underwear, and subjugated to the corporate pee-ons who take year-round vacations while he's forced to do data entry for eternity. What goes around comes around.

2. *Nutritional expert know-it-all*—Her personality has been touched on but not fully penetrated, if ever. She storms into the office, huffing and puffing, sweat dripping from her brow. She claims to have worked out, but everyone suspects her exhaustion was caused by the trip up the office stairs following a bacon, egg, and hash brown breakfast. Extra bread and carb-loading, always. Fortunately for anyone who suspects such a thing, she is a leading expert in all areas of nutrition, the smartest human in the history of the world (just ask her), and puts nothing unhealthy in her extremely large frame. Gluten-free? That's her! Caloric intake? She's a human calculator! Non-GMO? You betcha! Cell integrity? She can educate! How you should be eating? Just ask! Even if you don't ask, she will still give a nutritional seminar most days of the week and twice on Sundays. How does she do it? How does the nutritional expert maintain her defensive lineman physique while only allowing holy divinity into her body? No greater secret has been kept since Roman times and perhaps none ever will again. However, I know that she knows that I know her secret. I have refrained from letting the cat out of the bag until now, but the world must know. Truth be told, while the average corporate employee sleeps (in anticipation of an 8:00 a.m. start to the workday), nutritional expert know-it-all is up and at 'em, stuffing her face with hot dogs, macaroni and cheese, Bon-Bons, frozen burritos, sour candy, and all the gluttonous edibles she publicly declares should be banned by the federal government. I have seen the wizard of nutritional Oz, and that beast of a woman can eat!

3. *Queen of Hysteria*—Any time she speaks, everyone collectively holds their breath. Anxiety fills the room. Her voice is pure shrill. She has the nervous laugh of a lunatic, compounded by the physical and mental burden of every medical ailment known to man. She just got out of surgery, she needs surgery, her migraines are acting up, she can't

sleep, it is too hot outside yet too cool inside, her boyfriend is sick and doesn't work, her allergies are acting up, her face itches, she has an upset stomach, she can only eat certain foods, and on and on. The list grows daily. The queen of hysteria is predictably unpredictable; you never know what her problem of the day will be, but you can be damn certain the office will hear it. A beast at her desk, this woman growls, grunts, moans, shrieks, and pounds her keyboard with severe force over the frustrations of daily tasks. Although her job duties remain stagnant, Queen of Hysteria reacts with shock and awe at having to do a task she has performed in her job role the past ten years. Who the hell hired this woman, one may ask? Has California become so litigious that a maniacal woman cannot be fired without the company facing legal action? For every asshole manager, there is at least one queen of hysteria. For all the hype surrounding illegal discrimination and firing in corporate America, the queen of hysteria changes everyone's perspectives. After working with this cartoon caricature employee, not only would one support a liberal firing policy, they would march in favor of capital punishment for hysteria-driven employees who act in such a manner. In fact, Queen of Hysteria's peers frequently contemplate putting a hit out for her on Craigslist, and if they would get away with it. Anyone and everyone on the queen's floor would love to see an office beating, tire-iron style, à la Nancy Kerrigan in the 1994 Winter Olympics. "Why, whyyy?" Unfortunately, the government and lawyers have created a system of fear, where everyone is afraid to fire someone with a medical condition, no matter how fake or contrived it may be. The queen of hysteria will forever occupy the corporate workforce until she is either killed or retires claiming disability on her own accord.

4. *Blow-jobber*—"Excuse me, Mr. C-Level Executive, but can I give you a reach-around with that sloppy one?" This man

will pull out all stops to brown-nose any higher-ups in the company. Simultaneously, he will sabotage anyone who gets between him and his cozy role as biggest *blow-jobber* in the history of corporations. In meetings, he will offer blatant and unnecessary praise to his superiors. He will tattletale if anyone makes a decision without running it by upper management. Every idea that originates from execs, he adamantly commits to and praises, even if it is stale and outdated. The *blow-jobber* blindly follows wherever the shepherds of corporate business may lead. While he dedicates an hour each day going into his boss's office for a heavy brown-nosing session, this man is easily poised to give another four to eight hours of relentless ass-kissing, day in and day out. You walk by the boss's office in disbelief at the success the *blow-jobber* has in his tactics. The boss is laughing like an elementary schoolchild, obviously loving every second of worship bestowed upon them. They share secrets, inside jokes, and even go to lunch together as buddies. Are they gay for one another? Is this a real-life episode of *Brokeback Mountain*? Do these grown men discreetly enjoy men behind their wives' backs? Yes, they do.

5. *Patronizing Patty*—The woman talks down to you even when doing her a favor or fixing mistakes she made. She lacks knowledge of the company's systems, constantly screws things up, and then places blame on another department or individual without missing a beat. It is uncanny that she is able to pull it off without someone in upper management taking notice. Her ability to shift blame and smell like roses after fucking up a situation is due to one trait—the condescending tone of her voice. Patronizing Patty talks to everyone like their sole purpose in corporate life is to serve her every whim. Peers are viewed as peasants, hired to pamper her butt with white baby powder. She will argue until blue in the face, even when she is knowingly wrong. The woman never throws in the towel and sounds

like she wins every debate simply by talking to her opponent as one would a two-year-old.

6. *The token employee*—Before frothing-at-the-mouth liberals get their pink panties in a bunch, this is a term that can be applied to anyone, of any race. It can also be used without referencing race or ethnicity at all. Yes, we can take the issue head-on and say "token + insert race," but just as easily say "token douche bag." If we can't poke fun at everyone equally, then what the hell kind of world is this? Two words essentially define someone being token—unremarkable and expected. The token may or may not be a product of affirmative action. Token white boy comes into the office with an aura of arrogance, driving the BMW Daddy just got him, and acting like the man of the hour because he knows his dad's best friend, also the CEO, would never allow him to get fired. He attended USC—better known among non-elites as the University of Spoiled Children. He wears penny loafers, openly talks about how rad his weekend party was, and has a perpetual look of disbelief on his face. Some call it duckface; others call it douchebag look. Either way, this AC Slater type from *Saved by the Bell* is not doing himself any favors by acting like Mr. Cool Guy in the office. Last, but definitely not least, is the token affirmative action employee. It may be because of gender or race, but everyone knows the final decision to hire this employee was not because of talent alone. They just don't seem to get things as quickly as everyone else in the office. Their thinking is out loud and far from complex, but nobody can say anything for fear of sounding discriminatory. If you or anyone else made the same comments, you would be shut down and walked all over like a buffoon. Fortunately for affirmative action employee, they can get away with it.

7. *The over-underachiever a.k.a. the contextually blind*—Sometimes in business, you have to deem an appropri-

ate level of cutoff when making a decision. Oftentimes expedience is more important than exploring every detail to a ridiculous level of minutiae that bogs down the decision-making process. It is essentially the 80–20 (cost-sensitive) vs. 100 (waste-oblivious) rule. It is usually better to be 80 percent there and 20 percent uncertain for a decision than to take the time to be 100 percent right and waste time, money, and valuable resources. For example, you may lose out on purchasing discounts if you can't decide on a forecast, price increases may take effect due to inflationary forces, vendors may not be able to deliver on time, and you may end up with top products on backorder for peak selling season if a company acts indecisively. Don't tell this to the over-underachiever. This motherfucker thinks he is being the smartest guy in the room by never allowing a decision to be made without asking a million more questions than what is appropriate prior to taking action. Usually, this person was entitled growing up and has an inflated sense of self because of family background, not real-world experience. They read somewhere in a book that asking questions and challenging employees is key to success. The problem is they never understand the context of when to apply this approach and when enough is enough. Anyone who worked their way through business knows a company doesn't need to perform a comprehensive due diligence to decide whether or not to make a minuscule change to a company's website every time. If something looks like shit, change it on the spot. It doesn't require testing multiple versions and taking time to set up a comprehensive study. Change that shit. Change it now. Don't even think twice. Don't puff your chest up and believe you're being the smartest guy in the room. You look like an asshole over there, Mr. Over-Underachiever. Stop wasting time, money, and your own credibility trying to go above and beyond because it worked in certain instances for leaders in entirely different situations. Get a clue. Get in touch with reality and be contextually in tune with each unique situation. We know being accustomed to getting everything you wanted growing up, playing God in the office comes naturally, but this must stop now! Wild goose chases to satisfy every whim do nothing for growing the company's top (or bottom) line. Time is of the essence and costs are constantly creeping. Don't lead the company down a rabbit hole of costly, unnecessary measures. Sometimes less is more, unless we're talking titties (for guys) and wang size (for girls).

8. *Tits McGee (What's-her-role again?)*—Whoever made this hire is a complete pervert. Everyone in the office knows she wanders around doing little to nothing besides, of course, looking great. When you ask her a question, you forget its original intent because her response is so sexually provocative. It makes you think she may be desiring to do you right there on the spot. Don't get ahead of yourself. She deploys this tactic to everyone. In her job interview, she mesmerized male after male, convincing them to hire someone whose sole purpose in the office is to be eye candy and keep morale high. She walks around dressed to perfection and smelling like the cleanest flowery, sexual flavor known to man. One would floss with her thong and not think twice. She is that incredibly hot and hygienic. Women employees all talk shit, and males swoon while Tits McGee manages to stay saucy. She works in sales or marketing, but nobody really knows if she has a legitimate position in the company. Is her job sustainable? Across countless corporations worldwide, it sure seems to be. If you weren't born with boobs, ass, and a mouth to make men melt, maybe you should focus on being good at a technical skill. This job isn't for everyone, but Tits McGee is great at what she does.

9. *Constant Comedian*—They didn't quite make it in stand-up comedy, instead opting for a career in business. There are

varying degrees of how funny Constant Comedian can be from business to business. At worst, they make inappropriate, ill-timed, asinine comments in meetings. Blatant mood kill. At best, they lighten up the atmosphere with hilarious, subtle, perfectly delivered comments relevant to the topic being discussed. This joker may even add some insight into business matters with a humorous outlook that shines truth onto different areas of corporate operations. While busy dropping jokes, adding humor, and avoiding reporting on what they are expected to discuss, others are smiling—very awkwardly. It isn't normal employee behavior to act as such, and Constant Comedian does lose a certain amount of credibility. People start to feel one isn't doing a job as they don't discuss it much. Constant Comedian ends up embedding themselves in a Venus flytrap that hinders corporate progression—unless the CEO embraces humor. Most don't. Just a heads-up.

10. *Napoleon, not dynamite*—Everyone knows about Napoleon (syndrome), the little short guy trying to overcompensate by preemptively starting twenty-first-century office wars. The guy may even allude to throwing grenades, referring to suppliers as "Charlies" or "the enemy." He exudes insecurity. At any given time in any given room, he is the shortest guy there. Napoleon sports shoes with thick soles, inserts Dr. Scholl's cushions for an added half inch, but the little fella just can't seem to break 5'6". The thing is, if he wasn't so obsessed with height, he may be a better person. Instead, his focus is on proving there is a package in his pants, maybe larger than the general population of grown men of his physical height. Women all know that's not the case. He whines and reacts with unnecessary defense to any routine corporate situation. Napoleon's insecurities shout hysteria like Queen of Hysteria, but that woman is a bona fide psycho. Napoleon is just short. Napoleon received a truth bomb in his annual review, "You know, Napoleon,

> everyone in this office is sick of your projected insecurities. They interfere with your ability to interact as a normal professional would. To resolve this, we highly recommend that you get a penis implant. John Bobbet had one after Loren cut his off and threw it in the bushes off the freeway. The guy ended up in porn. You have options, but the current version of yourself is unfit for a career in business." The end, of small wang syndrome.

The list of cartoon character employees could continue to infinity and beyond. The truth is, we all have a cartoon character aspect to our personality. They may not be as extreme as some of those described above, but nobody is perfect. Even perfection can be a disparaged character trait. Never seem above everyone, and don't stoke the fire of jealousy among other employees. The point is, as one enters corporate life, people will take note of your every action. They will monitor when you come to the office, how you dress, the tone of your voice, actions, presented work, scent, bathroom breaks, significant other's looks, where you live, your friends, the car you drive, your personality, things you say, and anything else that opens a chance to talk smack. Be self-aware. Be cognizant of your personal shortcomings. If you are going bald, shave yo' head ASAP! If you have a perspiration problem, get some medicated deodorant. If you are fat, get on a treadmill or staple your stomach. If you are OCD, release it at home, then force yourself to be normal from eight to five. If you tend to be negative, slap a smile on your face and wear it all day long. If you aren't a details person, force yourself to dive into the minutia until it's uncomfortable. If you are lost in detail, take time to step back and absorb something bigger than minuscule ants. Look for the big-picture ant farm, operating in a methodical way. Don't allow yourself to be caricatured in your professional life. Show up and act. Yes, act. Act like you aren't that insecure kindergartner with a terrible haircut, shitty outfit, and fat legs showing up on the first day of school. It is obvious you are that person, but throw complexes out the door and become a consummate professional. Your career depends on it.

Chapter 3

I FINANCIAL-*ACCOUNTINGED* MY PANTS

IT HAS BEEN ALL FUN AND GAMES up to this point. We talked some shit, bashed simpletons who perform erroneous analysis, and listed the top ten biggest weirdos encountered in corporate America. This is where ish gets serious. This is when most of you zone out, cry wolf about hating math, and go into a cave of shame like a stack of patty cakes. Rejoice! You will soon realize that anyone can apply fundamental financial concepts to personal and business matters. You may already be doing it without any cognitive awareness. It is not all fun and games, but I am going to start by giving different examples of financial management that may help those who hate the thought of managing numbers. For the haters, maybe you can get on board after seeing fundamental business finance through the lens of a petty weed dealer at a college campus.

Okay, Mr. Big Shot. You not only made it to top-tier Claremont Colleges, but you figured out how to hustle through summers, keep the car constantly fueled, have a steady supply to get high, and even buy a new toy here and there from slanging. You, my man (*woman, tranny fanny, or gender nonbinary person*), have discovered marijuana as a selling commodity. Everyone loves that green exotic plant that, like a girlfriend, will lead you through all the different stages of any intense relationship. When you first discover her, there is that feeling of excitement and anticipation of the unknown. Thoughts race across your mind. *How good will she make me feel? I wonder where we will do it again and using what devices? Will it be better than the last time?* Damn, she makes me tired, lazy, and hungry. Should I fuck around with her friends or stay loyal to her? Marijuana is a very exciting new girlfriend. But like most women, she can run you for a lot of money; that is, unless you turn that babe into a moneymaker.

Petty drug dealing is a black-market operation. But like any business, the foundation rests within the three basic financial statements. Any operation will have some form of an income statement, balance sheet, and statement of cash flows. To understand how the three interact, you will need to be aware of the double-entry accounting model that was initially recorded by a Florentine merchant in thirteenth-century Italy.

In the double-entry method, any accounting transaction is recorded in a journal that rolls up into a general ledger of defined accounts. These accounts give a view into a company's financial health and performance by category. The three financial statements are derived from what is recorded in a company's accounting system via journal entries. Usually, a bookkeeper or accounting clerk will do this sort of tedious recording day to day. The general ledger acts as the backbone of a company's accounting system. Any time a transaction takes place, it is recorded twice, as a debit to one account and a credit to another. Rolling up to the basic accounting equation, these transactions will hit one financial statement as a debit and another as a credit. Every time you have a debit, you must have a credit. To further blow your mind, a debit can mean an increase or decrease, depending on what account it hits on the books. Get it? Got it. Good!

Before you *shart* your pants, let us get back to drug dealing. What exactly does double-entry accounting mean for a dealer? Let us pretend the Claremont College petty pot dealer is using a double-entry accounting method to manage his weed operation. When Mr. Dealer-Pot Head McFawker takes $4,000 and purchases a pound of grade-A blueberry chronic, his cash money is converted to weed (now an asset), literally and on the accounting books. In the most basic form, his entry is logged as a debit to merchandise inventory (an increase) in the amount of $4,000 and a credit (decrease) to cash for $4,000. Of course, we could set up a depreciation schedule for weed as an asset. That would entail allocating the cost of chronic over its useful life, making the accounting entry slightly more complex. But since weed is a high-velocity business, we will simplify for now. For businesses where an asset is used over the course of a few years, depreciation schedules make sense. For example, if you have a Scooby-Doo and Shaggy Stabbin' Wagon as your delivery mobile, a business vehicle is a common asset to use for depreciating the expense over the course of a few years (or its useful lifespan).

It is important to note that debits and credits can mean an increase or decrease depending on what part of the accounting equation they hit. Do not think a credit is always an increase and a debit is always a decrease. Review the paragraph above. For assets, a debit is an increase and a credit is a decrease. It does not sound or seem right, but it is! For a quick reference on how debits and credits hit each piece of the accounting equation, continue on below:

The Basic Accounting Equation

For Publicly Traded Companies
Assets = Liabilities + Stockholder's Equity

or

For Privately-Held Companies
Assets = Liabilities + Owner's Equity

To comprehend how journal entries impact each piece of the most basic accounting equation, let us start simple and progress. A fundamental and very first observation to the accounting equation is that the formula must balance, and so must all journal entries. Your assets must equal your liabilities added to owner equity. Your journal entries can be multiple for a single transaction, but all debits must equal credits, or it will throw your books off.

Assets	
Dbt	Cr
+	-

=

Liabilities	
Dbt	Cr
-	+

+

Equity	
Dbt	Cr
-	+

Look at "Assets" above. As you can see, a debit to assets results in an increase to an asset account, and a credit results in a decrease to a given asset account. You can see how debits and credits impact each part of the most basic view of the accounting equation as you scroll left to right.

Apply the equation above to understand what is going on below. It is sort of like getting in a girl's pants. You have to have a basic idea of what is going on in her head before putting your hand down her pants. No one wants to be a Harvey Weinsteiner with a #MeToo all over his or her face on social media. As a drug dealer, when you purchase a pound from a supplier, your $4,000 cash is converted to an asset (inventory) on the balance sheet. In addition, below is how the transaction would look as a journal entry. Whatever software you are using, it would be entered in some sort of format per below.

Date	Account Title and Description	Debit	Credit	Financial Statement(s) Affected
4/20/2018	Inventory	$4,000		Balance Sheet: Inventory is an asset (Debit = Increase)
	Cash		$4,000	Balance Sheet: Cash is an asset (Credit = Decrease)

**Bought 1 lb. of chronic with $4,000 cash*

If you are in the mindset of a moneymaker, you already foresee that the $4,000 purchase for chronic ballooning into a higher amount of cash. Naturally, you not only understand the chronic is an asset to your business, but it is also an asset on your balance sheet, one of the three financial statements. Businesses manage their accounting using journal entries like that above. Just like girls do not like superficial clitoral stimulation alone, you may need to go deeper to hit that G-spot for understanding the complexities of accounting. Understand that within each aspect of the accounting equation below, underneath Debit (DBT) and Credit (DBT), the plus (+) and minus (–) signs mean an increase or decrease to those accounts when you enter a DBT or CR.

Assets = Liabilities + Owner Equity										
Assets			Liabilities			Paid-In Capital			Owner's Draw	
Dbt	Cr	=	Dbt	Cr	+	Dbt	Cr	-	Dbt	Cr
+	-		-	+		-	+		+	-
*Cash			*Accounts Payables			*Or Common Stock			*Or Dividends	
*Inventory			*Rent							
*Accounts Receivables			*Invoices			Revenue			Expenses	
*Money Hoes Owe You			*Bills		+	Dbt	Cr	-	Dbt	Cr
			*Car Payments			-	+		+	-
			*Money You Owe Hoes							

Remember, remember the 5th of November, the accounting equation must always balance! All debits must equal all credits, *and* assets are always equal to liabilities plus owner's equity. Let's give a few examples as they apply to weed dealing. Now on the black market, there are no legal bindings, and risk gets priced into your business model. But for fuck's sake, let us pretend that a drug dealer was operating using business financials and accounting. Let's say that his legally binding contracts were that it was a "kill or be killed" marketplace. Instead of having legally binding, contractual obligations for accounts receivables (what women owe you) and accounts payable (what you owe to your papi) that the binding agreement was death. Essentially, you could put everything on the books like a normal business and possibly have to write off bad accounts if someone did not pay, but they would pay with their life. A wild concept, but let us flirt with this damn thing.

Example:

1. Your drug supplier from Tijuana "fronts you" (i.e., gives you weed without you having to pay up front) a pound of marijuana. However, you must pay him back. How does this affect the accounting equation?

Above example results in a debit to your assets account for merchandise inventory, the weed. If you look at assets in the chart above, a debit to an asset account means an increase, i.e., you debit (increase) an asset account for worth of merchandise inventory. Is that all? No. Why? Because all debits must equal credits, *and* the accounting equation must balance! Yes, assets are liabilities and owner equity. If we just left a debit (increase) to the asset account for the $4,000 worth of weed merchandise inventory, we would be out of whack. But the dealer fronted it with no cash exchanged. What the hell do you do?

Since you owe $4,000 to the dealer, that business transaction (him or her fronting you weed) hits the books as accounts payable. Look at the chart above. An accounts payable is a liability. It is a debt obligation you must pay. If not, you may lose your life, and all accounting and financial statement knowledge will not be worth shit. And since we already have a debit, you have to have a matching credit. You credit (meaning an increase) your liabilities account for accounts payables in the amount of $4,000 that you now owe and sits on your accounting books on the balance sheet. It all rolls back to the accounting equation. Going back to the weed man "fronting" you a pound, the accounting transaction looks per below.

Debit (increase) to Merchandise Inventory for $4,000. (Increase of Assets)

Credit (increase) to Accounts Payable for $4,000. (Increase of Liabilities)

Since assets equals liabilities and owner equity, you added $4,000 to both sides of the equation, so the accounting is solid. Your debit also matched your credits. Double-check. Let us examine how the petty pot dealer should understand each piece of the accounting equation. Below is a list of financial terms even an uneducated, hustler dealing drugs should know.

1. *Assets*—Weed for sale, scales, delivery vehicle, storage devices, and any other items owned by the dealer that produce economic value and could be converted to cash if needed.
2. *Current assets*—Those assets that could easily be converted to cash within a one-year timeframe. Weed and merchandise inventory would both be considered current assets since you can slang that product in a few weeks' time. Your "Shaggy, Scooby-Doo" mobile, which is worth less than you owe on it, would not be. This is because it would not be easy to convert a creeper van to straight cash, especially when you took out a loan to purchase it and have to pay it back monthly.
3. *Liabilities*—A liability could be that you owe a ganja grower four thousand dollars because he fronted you that pound on credit. The four thousand dollars would sit on the balance sheet as an account payable (liability). For real businesses, a liability must be a legal obligation, but we can bend a bit for this black-market operation. Since we are applying accounting and finance to drug dealing, let's consider any liability a blood obligation. You don't pay back, you could get killed, muchacho, like one of the jefes from the Netflix show *Narcos*.
4. *Paid-in capital*—You took money from the college fund, with no obligation to pay it back, and purchased a pound of weed to start slanging. That capital was paid in by the owner of the business to fund operations.
5. *Revenue (earned)*—You sell a few grams to customers. They can purchase on account, to be paid at a later time, or with cash handed over at the time of sale. Earned revenue is accrued at the time you fulfill or deliver your end of the bargain by providing marijuana. If you front any bozos

weed, then your revenue will still hit the income statement immediately, but the asset increase will be in the form of an account receivable instead of cash. Cash is king since some accounts receivable will have to be written off as bad accounts.

6. *Revenue (unearned)*—Stoner clients give you money, knowing you're about to hook up a new batch of Purple Diesel or some other strain with a ridiculous name. This exchange results in an asset increase to your balance sheet in the amount of cash they forked over, but your income statement does not see that revenue since you haven't fulfilled your end of the obligation and delivered the weed. This would be considered unearned revenue until you give them the chronic.
7. *Expenses*—Your weed business may incur expenses that are logged as journal entries and attributed to the income statement. For example, you purchase merchandise inventory (chronic) in bulk by the pound, fill up the car with gas for deliveries, buy a new scale, purchase petty dealer supplies (i.e., baggies and storage containers), and even host business meetings that deduct against your bottom line. In the real business world, some companies use expenses as a way to limit their income tax exposure to the government. For example, an accountant may say, "Fill up gas on your business card, expense meals that are business meetings," etc. That is because companies are taxed on net income, not revenue or topline sales. Expenses and shrinking net income for a real business can be a good thing if you consider tax implications. Since you are just a black-market dealer, expenses are all bad unless they grow your net income. Another major expense any operation can incur is inventory loss. This is paramount for illicit operations especially. If you are not tracking your inventory closely and lose some pounds here and there, you may have to write off that amount of your supply from inventory mer-

chandise (asset) as an expense (loss) to the income statement. Keep an eye on that supply.

8. *Retained* earnings—After everything is said and done, all investments in the company made, all weed purchased and sold for a given period, all expenses paid, and the income statement balanced out, this is the amount of money that is kept (retained) in the business. Think of retained earnings as the inverse of the money a pot dealer uses to buy toys and personal items. Instead of paying out the profits of the business to oneself, the money is kept on the books, making the business more valuable; although, that is not always the case. Real companies that pay dividends can be valued much higher than those that do not. If you have partners in your weed operation, they may expect a percentage of net earnings during a timeframe. The amount you pay to additional owners would be similar to dividends. The key is weed profits can be paid out (and subsequently used for personal purchases), divided up in any percentage among all owners (a la dividends), or retained and used only for business operations. Any drug dealer I have known usually prefers the former and neglects the latter options.

Now back to the bong. As you sell that stockpile of weed, accounting entries are made that hit the balance sheet, income statement, and statement of cash flows. For example, any time you sell an eighth of weed, the journal entries would be made per below (Table A). Table A may seem as foreign as ET "phoning" home, but understanding this makes the difference between thinking in terms of a business-savvy financial accountant and a simpleton. Table B is how everyone thinks of selling an eighth of weed on the day to day. Table B is also how you can think of a basic income statement and gross margins for a transaction in the most basic terms.

A) Journal Entries ➔ Single Transaction of Selling an eighth:

Date	Account Title and Description	Debit	Credit	Financial Statement(s) Affected
4/20/2014	Cost of Goods Sold	$31.25		Income Statement
	Merchandise Inventory		$31.25	Balance Sheet
**Sold weed that was purchased for $31.25 at cost (eighth = 1/128th of a pound at $4,000)*				
4/20/2014	Cash	$45.00		Balance Sheet, Statement of Cash Flows
	Sales		$45.00	Income Statement
**Sold an eighth of weed for $45 in cash.*				

B) Basic Income Statement or Gross Margin Review ➔ Single Transaction of Selling an *eighth*:

	Description	Amount ($ or %)	Notes
1	Revenue (Sales)	$45.00	Made a $45 sale for an *eighth* of weed.
2	Cogs (Cost of Goods Sold)	$31.25	Cost to buy weed was $31.25.
3	Gross Margin ($)	$13.75	Sales – Cost of Weed = Profit
4	Gross Margin (%)	30.56%	Gross Margin % = (Sales-Cost)/Sales

Why would a petty pot dealer go through the trouble of tracking transactions in the manner of Table A or Table B? For one, anyone who knows a pothead knows their memory is cloudy as a three-foot Jerome Baker bong, milked to the brim. The same goes for corporate executives, who are sometimes forgetful of details. For pot dealers, recordkeeping should also be paramount. Your clients are drug users; they obviously love the product you are selling, and this is not always a group of people whom you trust or know on a personal level. The person who owns the supply has a big target on their back in many ways.

For these reasons, the importance of the three financial statements (income statement, balance sheet, statement of cash flows) becomes crystal clear. The income statement allows you to know how profitable the business actually is after paying off expenses. As a petty pot dealer with an inflated sense of importance, one may be boasting a more profitable business than reality shows when the numbers are calculated. Are you giving out a lot of free or discounted weed? Do you have to drive great distances and spend a ton of money on gas to replenish your supply? Is your late-night post-bong-load eating habit (i.e., business meetings with clients) creating unnecessary business expenses? Are you overpaying for bulk chronic? Moreover, the biggest potential pitfall of dealing drugs is your dumbass getting so high off your own supply that you do not make much money. These questions are answered with honesty on the income statement.

The balance sheet is important to track the value of your assets and any liabilities you may need to pay off at a future date. Did you forget if you sold through a quarter pound of supply or was it a half pound? Do you continuously weigh your stash to ensure there is no inventory loss? Are you reconciling cash sales against the cost for that amount of weed? For any drug dealer, cash is king, but that cash likely is not being deposited into a bank or exchanged through many transactions. Even in illicit businesses, there is a vital necessity to track cash without flagging authorities and to have valid recordkeeping of how many greenbacks physically come in and go out of the operation. Cash is an asset. It sits on the balance sheet, but its value brings us to the third and final financial statement.

A statement of cash flows is intended to monitor, audit, and confirm cash amounts as cash physically moves from customer to cash register to bank to petty cash for business operations. Watch cash and any other transactional trip it may take along the way. The statement of cash flows also categorizes cash transactions as operating, investing, or financing activities. The real purpose is to, first, confirm the exact amount of cash a company has on hand and, second, to see if that cash available is sufficient to pay off bills and run the business. A statement of cash flows starts with a beginning balance, takes account of all cash transactions, and then arrives at an ending balance. If nothing adds up, a company is in big trouble, as cash is a target for embezzlement and fraud. This is one of the biggest problems that drug dealers face. If you are uber-successful and making millions of dollars running a black-market business, walk into a bank and ask to deposit under a new account. The Feds will come knocking at your door faster than you can ever financial-accounting your pants! Banks are extremely regulated and scrutinized by both internal and external auditors, but especially by the government. Ever watched a Netflix or Amazon Prime show and pretended to know what "money laundering" was but had no clue? Don't lie. Ask someone next time money laundering is mentioned, then hold your breath for a response. They will probably mention the "cleaning" of money in a dryer. Yeah, that may be part of it to erase any evidence of drugs on the currency itself. However, money laundering is a much more expansive term centered on finding illicit ways to get black-market cash back into a legal system of banks, businesses, etc., without having the FBI or DEA show up with their eager dicks dangling at the door. It puts things into a new perspective when you see random retail stores that one cannot fathom how they stay in business. Simple B School Bastardo rule: if the store has no transactional volume or business, it operates as a tax write-off for ultra wealthy folks because those businesses operate at a loss and reduce tax exposure. The other wild card scenario (and red-flag) is when a business operates on cash-only, does not accept credit cards, or looks suspicious in what it even does. But high-volume, high-velocity, and cash-only only businesses are the best to launder money back into the system by faking receipts, transactions, and pushing that drug money into the legal system. Cash is king but useless if you cannot spend it without going to jail.

Any person operating a weed operation should apply the overarching concepts of the three financial statements to effectively manage. Only publicly traded companies must report independently audited financial statements to the public. As a weed dealer, you do not have to be an expert at accounting entries, general ledger management, or financial statement analysis to effectively implement simple practices that can help with the success of one's operation. Pot may make you feel creative, deep, and euphoric, but number crunchers usually do not ace quantitative analysis tests while stoned. Everyone blazed in college, and your accountant may still. Black-market dealers usually do not come from a financial-accounting background. If this sounds like your situation and you do not plan to implement dual-entry accounting methodology to run a weed operation (please do not), at minimum understand and utilize the following from the three financial statements (income, balance sheet, cash flow):

Income statement considerations

1. *Recordkeeping*—Any time you have a business receipt, keep it and file it as revenue, expense, or purchase of an asset. For weed dealers, recordkeeping may not be the brightest idea from a legal standpoint (if the cops arrest you, this evidence will be used to incriminate you as a distributor), but if you want to manage the business's finances and its profitability, this is crucial. Furthermore, all it takes is a scale and some baggies to show distribution. Still, as a weed dealer, the best thing to do may be to have handwritten notes, unlabeled, showing numbers logged only, and using code words in place of known marijuana-related terms. Basically, take a finance book, copy the model for a business in terms of its revenues and expenses, and create a system that transfers to petty dealing. Do anything to make it look like the revenue and expenses are from a hypothetical business and not illicit dealings. With weed legalization sweeping across the great USA, the government will now expect cannabis companies to operate as normal companies. Many of you petty dealers may want to be in the ballgame, but you will have to understand real business concepts in order to stay viable.

2. *Max profit = good revenue – necessary expenses*—List out all revenues of the business in a given timeframe (backup with records if possible or you may forget) and subtract all expenses. This will give you an idea of profit. In a legitimate business, not all expenses are bad. You hear a lot about business meetings being *tax deductible.* That is because a business is taxed on its net earnings (revenue minus expenses or EBIT, earnings before interest and taxes). In the same tax

bracket, a business with higher net earnings will be taxed more than a business with less net earnings. If there are expenses a company owner likely would have accrued on his or her personal account anyway but can attribute to the business, it equates to killing two birds with one stone. The business "pays" for the meetings, and the company's tax liability is reduced because it shows smaller net earnings as that business expense is deducted from profitability (with profitability being what the government taxes). As a petty weed dealer, you now have the opportunity to pay legitimate taxes and use *safety sessions*[1] as tax-deductible business meetings in Colorado, California, Nevada, and many other states. Think of getting clients high as they come by and chill while picking up a Sativa-Indica hybrid. It is a small expense that yields a positive result, as people like free weed. This "business expense" acts as a promotional expense. You have a budget for it. Track it. Not all revenues are good, and not all expenses are bad. How can that be? Some revenues are bad if they come in the form of an account receivable; in other words, someone pays with an IOU. You have delivered your good or service (weed), thus earning revenue, but they have yet to pay cash to the business. Thus, you collected revenue, but not a cash asset—rather, an account receivable asset that sits on the balance sheet. If this IOU is from a shady character, it is a classic example of bad revenue. If that person never pays, you have to write off that account receivable as a "loss." The accounting entry would hit the balance sheet and income statement simultaneously. Whereas your revenue looked good when you delivered it, the asset (account receivable IOU) became a loss on the books entirely. Conversely, some expenses are healthy and necessary to grow the business (as in the case of blazing out clients). In legitimate (and now legal cannabis) companies, expenses take away tax liability, as government taxes

[1] Marijuana smoking sessions

are based on net earnings. At the end of the day, common sense will determine whether or not an expense is wasteful spending and the appropriate risk in earning revenue via accounts receivable. That is why some leaders with little or no financial knowledge are successful entrepreneurs. They have common sense, even in the drug-dealing world.

3. *Timeframe for reporting*—The income statement will act as a baseline for anyone to manage profitability. As a business, the timeframe for reporting on net earnings is key, such as daily, monthly, quarterly, and annually. It is amazing that some businesses do not understand the concept of appropriate timeframe comparison for reporting. You must always compare year-to-date vs. prior year (same timeframe) and current period (quarter, month, and week) vs. previous year(s), same period to get the full picture. Some companies will only use comparisons *vs. prior period.* This makes no sense if you are comparing your slowest time of year to the prior period which was the busy season. For proper forecasting and management, a financially savvy leader must understand seasonality, trends within the industry, and real growth comparison calculations. Anyone out there wonder why the biggest shopping/sale day of the year is called Black Friday? It is traditionally known as the day when companies get "out of the red" and "into the black."[2] As a legal cannabis distributor in California, timing has been everything since its inception as a state-legal business model. Every person with money to spare on the planet decided to invest in marijuana supply, leading to a tremendous drop in prices, the ouster of once-prosperous, small-time black-market distributors and even a scenario where a bag of Mary Jane is cheaper to buy than it is to produce. Timing is never going to be an exact science, but understanding timeframes for comparison will

2 Red signifying a financial negative (or loss) and black signifying a financial positive (or positive earnings)

help with inventory planning, purchasing, discounting, and managing sales velocity, as seasonality can vary across different industries. Do you think sunscreen sales peak in winter or summer in California? Do marijuana sales peak in winter or summer? Check your sales records and analyze by week, month, quarter, and year. Leverage all timeframes available, and make notes of any catastrophic, adverse events that may have influenced previous years (floods, fires, natural disasters, loss of ability to transport, etc.). Maybe sales stay consistent, but the distribution model changes, as a business is required to make more deliveries during a certain time of year. Maybe a customer base shifts during certain periods of the year from beachgoers to mountain-goers. Retail pump gas prices rise during summer as consumption peaks, but electric bills tend to peak during winter as demand for indoor heat mounts. Businesses need to understand themselves thoroughly by analyzing supply and demand with proper reporting timeframes for income statements and forecasting analyses. This sticks for any business.

4. *Categorization of revenue and expenses*— As a data analytics doucher (me) who has performed everything from financial to customer segmentation to operational to sales to cost analyses, a key component of this job entails looking at data and being able to appropriately categorize and attribute metrics to appropriate areas of the business. If you have a sophisticated accounting system, it will force you to categorize each journal entry. If you are in the process of getting there or slinging marijuana, you likely do not have these luxuries in place yet. It is easy to go through and categorize your revenue and expenses in an Excel spreadsheet and line up expenses against the revenue they earn. For example, if you are slanging pot brownies as part of your weed operation, look at the total revenue brought in from that line and subtract out the cost of all ingredients that go into those edibles, and then determine profitability. Do the

same for your different types of weed. It will help guide you in the direction of maximizing profitability and rallying the company around its core competencies, i.e., analysis will allow a company to see what it does best and run with it. It also shows where there are opportunities for improvement. Look at what competitors are doing. See how they categorize on e-commerce and promote. There is a world of data, but if you cannot organize it properly, it is useless. No two businesses or industries are identical. Take a step back and determine exactly how you want your business to be dissected. Then manage to how that puzzle looks.

5. *Uniformity of reporting*— One of the biggest issues with potheads is they deal across multiple units of measurement depending on the amount of weed a user wants to buy. It is never good to be dealing across multiple metrics. For engineering, a machine isn't built using half metric and half inch-pound systems. An Audi dealer doesn't have the tools to work on an American-made Chevrolet, and vice versa for the Chevrolet mechanic. Audi is German-made, meaning the tools are in metric. Chevrolets are made using customary units, a traditional unit of measurement leftover and evolved from Britain. In America, there is a tendency and tradition of mixing it up with measurements. We measure our height in feet and inches and our football fields in yards. Maybe the pothead tradition of using grams alongside ounces and pounds came to be via a Mexican (metric units) and American (customary units) going into cannabis distribution together while stoned. Some units stuck from the Mexican, and others from the American, so we now mix ounces (customary) with grams (metric) for common street nomenclature. See below for the traditional street measurement of common increments for selling weed (highlighted in black) and its weight converted to other metrics. As a business, pick one and gc for it, but be consistent when calculating transactions. Grams and kilograms would seem

to make the most sense, but they are difficult to conceptualize as an American growing up with pounds and ounces. However, you must be able to perform the conversions from one to the other at any given time, as to be agile and intelligent. Think of it like spending money in a foreign country: would you go on a shopping spree, not knowing how many Chilean pesos are equal to an American dollar? No. Study conversion calculations and be able to perform the math below. The "Common Name" is what the American streets are used to, but look at the weight in metric vs. customary. Uniformity will play a key role in reporting for cannabis as the legalized market blossoms.

Common Name	Weight in Grams (Metric)		Weight in Ounces (Customary)		Weight in Pounds (Customary)		Street Name
Dime Bag	1 / 2	gram	1 / 56	ounces	1 / 896	pound	*Dime, Dime Bag*
Gram	1	grams	1 / 28	ounces	1 / 448	pound	*Gram, Grr, G, Goober*
Half Eighth	1.75	grams	1 / 16th	ounces	1 / 256	pound	*Half Eighth, Ry-Todd*
Eighth	3.5	grams	1 / 8th	ounces	1 / 128	pound	*Eighth, 8 Ball, 8'er*
Ounce	28	grams	1	ounces	1 / 16	pound	*O, O-Z, O-Zer*
Quarter Pound	112	grams	4	ounces	1 / 4	pound	*QP*
Half Pound	224	grams	8	ounces	1 / 2	pound	*Half*
Pound	448	grams	16	ounces	1	pounds	

Calculations above are based on 28 grams to an ounce (not exact), when there are actually 28.3495 grams per ounce. You may have been getting short-changed this entire time thinking 28 grams was an ounce, depending on the scale's metric used!

6. *Gross margin*—One of the most important financial measures for any selling product will be its gross margin. Gross margin is the percentage of revenue that is profit after subtracting out cost of goods sold. See below for a chart showing both gross margin dollars and gross margin percentages for the most common selling increments of a cannabis

dealer who purchased a pound of weed for $4,000. It is important to note that gross margin does not include all costs of the business. For example, to sell this weed, one may have had to drive to their customers and spend gas money. That is reflected on the income statement under operating expenses. One may have to pay salaries and rent to run the business. These costs would be viewed under salary expense and rent expense, appropriately, on the income statement. Gross margin is product-cost specific, while net income statement gives a whole view of the business. Please review gross margin table below. You will note that oftentimes businesses give "price breaks" if someone buys in larger increments (i.e., they charge less per unit if you purchase more). Why would they utilize this strategy? Look at the far right column and how much their gross margin percentages decline. They are thinking in the short-term and the column right next to it, "margin dollars." While the transaction of selling a pound for $4,750 nets only a 15.8 percent gross margin, the dealer is making $750 off that transaction. A street savvy businessperson considers both margin dollars and margin percent when slanging.

				$4K for a pound		= (Price - Cost) /Price
Common Name	Weight in Grams		Selling Price	Dealer Cost (Cogs)	*Margin Dollars*	*Gross Margin Percent*
Dime Bag	1/2	gram	$10	$4.46	*$ 5.54*	*55.4 percent*
Gram	1	grams	$20	$8.93	*$ 11.07*	*55.4 percent*
Half Eighth	1.75	grams	$25	$15.63	*$ 9.38*	*37.5 percent*
Eighth	3.5	grams	$45	$31.25	*$ 13.75*	*30.6 percent*
Ounce	28	grams	$350	$250.00	*$ 100.00*	*28.6 percent*
Quarter Pound	112	grams	$1,350	$1,000.00	*$ 350.00*	*25.9 percent*
Half Pound	224	grams	$2,500	$2,000.00	*$ 500.00*	*20.0 percent*
Pound	448	grams	$4,750	$4,000.00	*$ 750.00*	*15.8 percent*

7. *Markup*—Markup is a more common sales term and metric for retail operations. Companies usually manage to a gross

margin percent because it is easier to conceptualize and apply to making a business profitable. Markup can be an important measurement to close a sale or make the case to a customer who is weary of how much a dealer is charging. It all depends on the situation, as sometimes a weed dealer may not want to show his hand to clients for fear of the unknown. I have always felt transparency is the best policy for customers because it promotes trust between the two parties. Markup is essentially saying what percentage a seller has marked up a product over its cost. This helps consumers conceptualize how much they are paying to purchase from the dealer versus getting it from the dealer's dealer. As is the case with most businesses, they will give a slight discount (or smaller markup) if the customer purchases larger quantities. That is because they are getting more margin dollars in total as they sell larger increments. Their biggest markup, or highest margin percentage item below, would be selling a dime bag or gram according to the table.

			$4K for a pound	= (price - cost) / cost
Common Name	Weight in Grams	Selling Price	Dealer Cost (Cogs)	Markup
Dime Bag	1/2 gram	$10	$4.46	124.0 percent
Gram	1 grams	$20	$8.93	124.0 percent
Half Eighth	1.75 grams	$25	$15.63	60.0 percent
Eighth	3.5 grams	$45	$31.25	44.0 percent
Ounce	28 grams	$350	$250.00	40.0 percent
Quarter Pound	112 grams	$1,350	$1,000.00	35.0 percent
Half Pound	224 grams	$2,500	$2,000.00	25.0 percent
Pound	448 grams	$4,750	$4,000.00	18.8 percent

Balance sheet

8. *Inventory management, physical* audits—Any business, of any type, should understand the importance of physical inventory audits. A current asset is the closest thing to cash

a business has. If that current asset is inventory, it must be treated like cash. If inventory is being embezzled or a company is losing its inventory via mismanagement or loss, it is the equivalent of throwing cash down the drain. Listen up, Mr. Pothead Fucker. You take that supply of Purple Diesel you're slangin' in eighths and grams, weigh that out, and audit it against how much you've sold! Your roommate, girlfriend, or even best friend may be pinching off your supply, acting as a drain on the profitability of your business. You will replenish that weed supply more often, with less cash money, than if that Mary Jane was sold for Benjamins (instead of smoked by your hippie-ass girlfriend). Periodic physical inventory counts are crucial for any business. If your counts are off, you must increase the frequency of how often you perform them.

9. *Working capital*—A typical balance sheet differentiates between current assets and long-lived assets. It does the same for liabilities. Current assets can easily be converted to cash within a one-year timeframe. Similarly, current liabilities are those that come due in one year or less. One key calculation for a company to monitor is how much working capital it has. Working capital is simply current assets minus current liabilities. It essentially allows a business to determine its ability to pay off any short-term debts and the remaining cash it could have after doing so. Another way to look at working capital is as a ratio: working capital ratio = current assets ÷ current liabilities. The importance of ratios is that a dollar amount of working capital does not tell the whole story. For example, positive working capital of $10,000 may sound like a lot, but it may or may not be, depending on the size of the business

and how those current assets are allocated. See below for two scenarios regarding working capital metrics:

Scenario 1, Claremont's Petty Dealer		
Current Assets		NOTES:
Cash	$10,000	*80 percent of American bills have cocaine residue, probably the most valuable part of American currency with $17 trillion in national debt!*
Inventories	$40,000	*10 lbs. at $4,000 per lb. (use COGS)*
Accounts Receivable	$500	*10 customers owe $50 each*
Total Current Assets	$50,500	*Easily convertible into cash within a one-year timeframe.*
Current Liabilities		
Accounts Payable	$40,000	*Supplier fronted you 10 lbs. at $4,000 per lb. You must pay this back ASAP.*
Account Payable	$500	*$500 cash loan from a buddy you needed to buy selling supplies and bongs to market the business.*
Total Current Liabilities	$40,500	*Total amount of debt you must pay (come due) within a one-year timeframe.*
Working Capital = Current Assets - Current Liabilities	$10,000	10,000 in working capital ain't all that bad for a petty dealer at a nerdy private school with 1,200 students.
Working Capital Ratio = Current Assets / Current Liabilities	1.25	You have 1.25 times the amount of current assets as current liabilities.

Quick Ratio = (Current Assets - Inventories)/ Current Liabilities	$0.26	For every $1 of debt, you have $0.26 to pay it off (considering your accounts receivables don't stiff you for moneys owed).

Scenario 2, The Importer		Notes:
Current Assets		
Cash	$50,000	Big ballin' with $50,000 all stacked in one-dollar bills, yo.
Inventories	$450,000	You paid $500,000 cash for a 250-pound shipment from Mexico. Unfortunately, you have only sold through $50,000 of that at cost, leaving you with $450,000 on the balance sheet.
Accounts Receivable	$10,000	Some scumbags owe you $10,000 for weed you fronted them.
Total Current Assets	$510,000	

Current Liabilities		
Accounts Payable	$500,000	You agreed to a second 250 lbs., $500,000 shipment from your Mexico supplier. You tell him you will have the cash next week and he agrees to deliver anyway.
Total Current Liabilities	$500,000	

Working Capital = Current Assets - Current Liabilities	$10,000	You are importing half a million dollars in weed at a time and still only have $10,000 in working capital? That ain't cuttin' the mustard!
Working Capital Ratio = Current Assets / Current Liabilities	1.02	Current asset to current liability ratio is almost 1:1. Not looking too good, Bob!

Quick Ratio = (Current Assets - Inventories)/ Current Liabilities	$0.12	For every dollar of debt, you only have $0.12 to pay it off cash on hand, or coming in (hopefully), to pay it off! You had better start moving that inventory. Weed rots, dumbass!

In the two scenarios above, $10,000 of working capital is not $10,000 of working capital for both the petty Claremont dealer (scenario one) and the drug importer (scenario two) operating on a larger scale. That is why additional capital metrics are important to gauge any business. Working capital alone can give you an idea of the amount of cash you could have in the short term to pay off short-term debt obligations. However, it does not put that potential cash into perspective or compare actual on-hand cash to short-term debt liabilities. For example, if you compare capital metrics for the petty dealer to the large-scale importer, they both have $10,000 of working capital, but the petty dealer has 1.25 times the amount of current assets as current liabilities versus a 1:1 ratio for the importer. Additionally, the Claremont dealer has $0.26 of short-term available cash (or payments that should come in) to pay off every $1 of debt. The importer only has $0.12 of cash to pay off every $1 of debt. For scenario two, when you have half a million dollars in debt obligations, that can be a very scary situation to be in. These are very simple, straightforward cases. As businesses become more complex and acquire financing through multiple sources (a mix of debt and equity), financial analysis needs to be more complex (and scalable) to paint the vivid picture.

Has the day already arrived when drug customers are paying with different payment methods such as cash, check, credit, invoice, and using terms such as 2%/15 net 30, 3%/30 net 60, etc.? I have not heard of drug dealers offering a 2% discount if a customer pays the full amount on a thirty-day invoice within fifteen days, but it may already have arrived with cannabis legalization in California. As a well-informed businessperson, it is important to know different payment scenarios and how they can affect a company's cash flow and ability to pay off debt obligations. Working capital is a financial concept that allows one to manage effectively.

10. *Cash flow and asset management*—This seems like an obvious one, but for some, it is not. I was helping a friend who owns and operates a small business, trying to find the underlying cause of where the money was going from their business and why they were not clearing more money. The first thing we did was go through and track, categorize, put into a timeframe, and analyze revenue against expenses. Since this was an operation where there were not many bad payment issues, we treated revenue mostly as cash. With that, we found the owner's purchasing flow was not in line with sales quantities on products. For example, the owner was spending as much on inventory each month as the sales. Upon further discussion, they were certain they were running out of product all the time and had to purchase the quantities that they were to fill demand. That meant inventory was being taken and/or sales were not being tracked. It turns out that it was a combination of both. Employees would take a product here, a product there; use it for business operations without ever accounting for it. They would give out discounts here, make a note they forgot to log as a sale there, and so on.

    As we continued down the road to find problem areas of the business, it turned out the cash drawer was not being accounted for daily, the bank account was consistently overdrawn, and the business was always short on cash. How does one resolve these issues? We agreed on a physical inventory count to let everyone in the business know that everything was being properly accounted for. Next, we agreed there would be a daily cash drawer count. Cash deposits would be audited and tracked. It turned out the owner's kids would come in and take $20 here, likely the cash drawer operator would do the same, the owner would take cash for spending, and at the end of the day, there was little cash left for the business. While this may seem obvious, cash management is one of the most important tools to manage in a business.

As a weed dealer, you likely will not be making cash deposits, so you cannot take your beginning balance and add in cash flow from operating, investing, and financing activities to arrive at an ending cash balance for that period. However, as a pot peddler, you can count your bills daily and audit against known sales and the amount of weed remaining on the balance sheet.

Asset Management (Inventory)		
Beginning Weed Balance	28	Grams
Sales	-10	Grams
Personal Use	-3	Grams
Ending Balance	15	Grams

Cash Management		
Beginning Cash Balance	$1,500	
Cash From Operating (Weed Sales)	$200	*Sold 10 grams at $20 each
Cash From Operating (Purchase of 1 Oz.)	$(300)	
Cash From Investing (Capex)	$(50)	*Purchased $50 bong to "test" supplies
Cash From Financing	$(50)	*Paid off an eighth you owed for
Ending Cash Balance	$1,300	

From simple reconciliation above, you can make sure you have $1,300 cash on hand and 15 grams of supply (weed inventory) remaining to sell. This does not take complex accounting or deep math skills. You do not even need to understand algebra to track the two most important pieces of your business, cash, and inventory. You just need to be able to track transactions and add and subtract. Most weed dealers do not deal with numbers or taking the time to physically count (weigh) supply. If you are not tracking cash or inventory, someone else is, and your inventory and cash audits could look more like this:

Asset Management (Inventory)		
Beginning Weed Balance	28	Grams
Sales	-10	Grams
Personal Use	-3	Grams
Friends Pinched	-3	Grams
Girlfriend Pinched	-2	Grams
Roommate Pinched	-2	Grams
Overweighed While Stoned	-1	Grams
Ending Balance	7	Grams

Cash Management		
Beginning Cash Balance	$1,500	
Cash from Operating (Weed Sales)	$200	*Sold 10 grams at $20 each
Cash from Operating (Purchase of 1 oz.)	$(300)	
Cash from Operating (Roommate Theft)	$(100)	
Cash from Operating (Lost While High)	$(50)	
Cash from Operating (Misplaced While High)	$(100)	
Cash from Operating (Girlfriend's Allowance)	$(200)	
Cash from Investing (Capex)	$(50)	*Purchased $50 bong to "test" supplies
Cash from Financing	$(50)	*Paid off an eighth you owed for
Ending Cash Balance	$850	

Running a business is not rocket science. As a business grows and becomes more complex, it may require additional expertise and perceptive management to stay successful. However, anyone can implement fundamental financial management practices that will allow him or her to thrive and be more aware of the overall health and performance of a company. If a weed dealer is wasting money and constantly coming up short when additional supply is needed, it is obvious that he or she is blowing through cash like a jackass. However, unless there is a recorded account of exactly how much and where that money is wasted, it will be difficult to right the ship. Numbers often allow people to face reality. They often confirm common sense. A dumbass pothead may act as if they are living on top of the world when, in actuality, their cash flow management barely allows them to keep the operation afloat. While throwing around wads of cash, the supplier may be fronting ounces at a time. The petty dealer sinks into a situation where they are scrambling every time accounts payable come due.

Do not fear the thought of financial management. Do not fear basic math and accounting. Do not fear catchphrases like "asset management," "cash flow," "reconciliation," or "audits." These simple financial catchphrases have been covered at a fundamental level in this chapter. They are the basics of finance that you can quickly deploy for the enhancement of your business. Whether you are a stoner, a petty pot dealer, a big-scale marijuana importer, or just an average dude or chick starting up a business, these are concepts to have as the baseline for every decision you make for the company. While I would not expect anyone to jump into the role of CFO with these newfound financial management tools, understanding them will allow you to relate to any shrewd CFO's root-level objectives. Baseline everything against the three financial statements, and you will be making decisions that can be backed up with strategy.

Now get back to your purple-lit room, turn down the Jimi Hendrix, pull out some hemp paper, and chicken scratch all the revenues and expenses your pathetic operation has incurred in the past month. Ready, set, toke! Just make sure to inhale, unlike that one president who sucked on Lewinsky-flavored cigars.

Chapter 4

CURRENCY, YOUNG BUCKS

IF YOU ARE A YOUNG BUCK (OR doe) reading this, you may be sitting there thinking your life goal is to save the world, feed the children, and all the mumbo jumbo BS Commie college professors indoctrinate into students' loins. Your idea of a job is likely one with deep "meaning" that makes your private parts tingly. I'd hate to blow up the lies, but the overwhelming majority of politicians and professors really only care about their own paychecks and pitch this nonsense so you vote to make their jobs more lucrative. On the other hand, if you have supported yourself without the help of mommy and daddy, then you may have scrutinized that paycheck and noticed a fifty-thousand-dollar salary per year does not mean you actually take home anywhere near that amount after the government's intervention. Thank your Commie professors and all others that conned you into voting for politicians to redistribute your paycheck! On top of it all, you get taxed on your paycheck, pay taxes to the IRS at the end of the year on your income (that was already taxed), pay sales tax on everything you buy, and then pay property taxes if you own a property. Throw in the DMV and all the fees levied anywhere you step, and taxes become an exponentially grand albatross against that fifty-thousand-dollar salary.

As I sit here and write this, I am nearly 2,900 miles from Washington, DC. I simply can't find it realistic that sending a large chunk of my paycheck there and another chunk to Sacramento is an efficient use of funds I personally earned. Hell, I look around, and the freeways in California are riddled with potholes that make me nervous every time I ride my motorcycle down Highway 101. If one of those potholes caused my tire to pop and result in my untimely death, the government would be immune from liability. If, on private property, someone knowingly had roads that posed a hazard, people entered their premises, and that trespasser crashed and injured themselves on those roads, that private property owner would be liable. That is the American legal system at its finest!

Something else that really irks me: in the news as of late, the business industry and finance sector, in particular, have been ostracized for their alleged greed. Similarly, conservatives who want lower taxes and less government regulation have also been labeled greedy mother fuckers by mainstream media. Ironically, the greediest group of all—power-hungry politicians who constantly want to take and spend your money—are portrayed as socioeconomic heroes, saving society's disadvantaged.

This is where a few examples and economics 101 need to come into play. Conceptually, a true free market is an agreement between two parties to exchange goods and/or services for the goods and/or services that another man or woman provides. Since, say, an oil driller in North Dakota may have no need for the goods and/or services provided by a hemp farmer in Kentucky, there becomes a need for a currency that allows an economy to surpass the limitations of the barter system. In a barter system, two participants exchange goods in their physical possession. If you are strictly a wheat producer but need chicken eggs from a guy or gal who is already stocked up on wheat, then you would be shit out of luck. This is the barter dilemma, which leads to one of two solutions: (1) a commodity becomes the economy's effective currency (such as silver or actual gold coins being exchanged), or (2) a currency becomes backed by a commodity (such as when the US dollar was backed by gold or sacks of grain equated to coins in Ancient Egypt). The last solution, and what we have in America for the most part, is a fiat currency, with its strength coming from oil transactions being mostly settled using American dollars, which gives it value. However, danger exists in this situation when the government prints money that has no intrinsic value and declares it as a medium of exchange.

Let's put the Kentucky hemp farmer and North Dakota oil driller exchange on paper and map it out: from the earliest stages of barter to an Ancient Egyptian-type system based on bushels of wheat to modern society's fiat currency exchange.

Barter system

In a true barter system, two market participants meet and negotiate how many pounds of hemp should be exchanged for a barrel of oil. This is a pure market. There are no other considerations aside from negotiation. There are minimal external market forces, no currency considerations, and the supply and demand is determined by how much hemp the farmer is willing to pay in exchange for barrels of oil and vice versa. Of course, this is never the full picture because Mr. Tax Collector would come around and coerce both hemp and oil producers into paying the government a portion of their production. The government may be closer friends to the hemp producer than to the oil producer and unfairly tax oil producers. This would then affect how much the oil producer is willing to accept in trade. With government intervention, not only is the oil producer getting screwed, but so is their trading partner, the hemp producer, as the cost to produce rises for both participants.

Commodity-backed currency

Let's go back to the Ancient Egyptian period when a bushel of wheat (roughly eight dry gallons) was the standard for settling trade transactions. Those bushels were used to settle payments; in other words, bushels backed the currency in the form of coins equaling different increments of wheat bushels. If you produced a crop of hemp or cannabis under this system, you would keep what you needed for personal use and trade it in for as many bushels of wheat as the exchange rate proved worthy. Essentially, the wheat bushel coins would be used as payment for all economic transactions.

Pretend we are living under the Ancient Egyptian currency system, running around with big old bushels of wheat as the commodity exchange rates are based upon. You can see below how the conversion for Kentucky hemp and North Dakota oil barrels relates to bushels of wheat.

	Measurement	Bushels of Wheat Equivalent
Kentucky Hemp	1 Pound	= 5 Bushels
North Dakota Oil	1 Barrel	= 100 Bushels

As a Kentucky hemp farmer, say you need a barrel of oil. Having never seen this mofo slanging that black gold North Dakota oil, and never having converted hemp to oil in previous transactions, some analysis is required. Upon meeting for the first time, knowing how valuable both assets (hemp and oil) are in terms of bushels of wheat, how would this transaction be settled? How many pounds of hemp do you offer in exchange for a barrel of oil? In the most basic form, from the hemp farmer's standpoint, you need to know what number times five equals one hundred. That will be the number of pounds (hemp) to equal one barrel of oil.

Any time a number is unknown, that number becomes the unknown variable in your algebraic equation. In this case, we don't know how many pounds of hemp you need to make one hundred bushels of wheat, or one barrel of oil. You do know that one pound of hemp is equal to five bushels of wheat and one hundred bushels of wheat is equal to one barrel of oil. To make things equal, you need to convert five bushels of wheat (equal to one pound of hemp) to one hundred bushels of wheat (equal to one barrel of oil). Can you pull a skin flute out of your bum and make it happen magically? Hell nah, you have to use algebra! Below is how we would work through this issue and any issue involving exchange rates and conversion from one metric to another. It becomes the basis of logic for problem solving.

Step-by-step logic

What is the dilemma? >>>	Hemp farmer needs a barrel of oil
List all known facts >>>	1 barrel of oil = 100 bushels of wheat
	1 pound of hemp = 5 bushels of wheat
What is the question to be solved? >>>	How many pounds of hemp for a barrel of oil?
	i.e., how many 5 bushel increments (pounds of hemp) do you need to make 100 bushels (1 barrel of oil)?
Write the equation and solve. >>>	1 barrel oil = 100 bushels (equal to 1 barrel of oil) divided by 5 bushels (per pound of hemp).
	i.e., 1 barrel of oil = 100 bushels of wheat / 5 bushels of wheat per pound of hemp = 20 pounds of hemp
	I.e. 5x=100 => x=100/5 => x=20
	20 pounds of hemp = 1 barrel of oil
Does this logic test out?	20 pounds of hemp × 5 bushels per pound = 100 bushels total.
	So 100 bushels of wheat = 1 barrel of oil = 20 pounds of hemp. Yes!
Always two ways to exchange >>>	What are the exchange rates for barrels of oil to pounds of hemp and vice versa?
Solved above	How many pounds of hemp = 1 barrel of oil? Solution: 20 pounds of hemp = 1 barrel of oil
Unknown	How many barrels of oil = 1 pound of hemp?
	1 pound of hemp = x barrels of oil
	20 pounds of hemp = 1 barrel of oil
	Divide both sides of equation by 20 to get 1 pound of hemp.
	20/20 = 1/20
	1 pound of hemp = 1/20 barrels of oil
	= 1/20 = 0.05 = 5 percent
	Solution: 0.05 barrels of oil = 1 pound of hemp
Does this test out?	1 barrel of oil = 20 pounds of hemp
	1 pound of hemp = 1/20 barrels of oil

MULTIPLIER	BARRELS OF OIL	POUNDS OF HEMP	BUSHELS OF WHEAT
1X	1/20th	1	5
5X	5/20th = 1/4th	5	25
10X	10/20th = 1/2	10	50
20X	1	20	100

Free market transactions and regulation

Okay, maybe I lost you with all those steps, variables, and conversions of two different commodities and measurements that you don't give a rat's ass about. Hemp has a connection to weed, but it may remind you of dirty hippies burning incense sticks and avoiding showers. You may even associate the smell of hemp with stinky-hippy armpits. Let's describe conversion into pothead terms the college kids will want to understand. Coming up is a different example than above and very important to comprehend the difference between a truly free market and a highly regulated one.

Let's explore the dynamic of weed on the black market vs. weed on the legalized, highly regulated American market. Recently, marijuana was legalized in Colorado for recreational use, opening up the doors for manufacturers and companies to go on the record for the production of marijuana and distribution without fear of state government coming in and arresting those involved. However, the Obama administration is still aggressively shutting down and prosecuting "legal" marijuana dispensaries in California, so there is still the omnipresent risk of a run-in with the FBI or DEA due to the conflict between state and federal laws on marijuana issues.

So we have a president who smoked weed in college but now sends different branches of government to shut down legal, medical dispensaries to ransack them for cash? Even when voters in California supported the use of marijuana for medicinal purposes? Hypocritical? Most definitely.

For all intents and purposes, there are legal risks for running a state-legal medicinal dispensary in California, a state-legal production and distribution center in Colorado, or a black-market operation in any of the two states. Risk for black-market, illegal operations is usually priced into the business model. Drug dealers charge a higher price and cushion margins because of the omnipresent possibility of ending up in jail running a black-market business. Weed dealers would be tough to come by if the industry wasn't rewarded with high-margin transactions. Think about it: how much would someone have to pay you to risk going to jail for a job? That cost of risk is built into the weed-dealing model, and people enter that market with money outweighing the peril of legitimate jail time.

When you think about a traditional drug-dealing model and widespread information available on the growing process, many potheads have access to a source dealer who both grows and sells the cannabis they consume. If an end consumer is buying in smaller increments, such as eighths or grams, they may be getting herbs through a distributor who adds a markup and builds margin into selling prices.

With the "legalization" (or "regulation and taxation") of recreational marijuana in Colorado, the government has decided upon a 15 percent wholesale tax and a 15 percent retail tax, on top of all costs associated with running a business (income taxes, employee and business taxes, permitting, etc.). These added costs of being a legitimate recreational seller of marijuana make your cannabis more expensive. What does this mean for Colorado stoners? Legal weed is a lot more expensive than black-market weed. It is a great example of how a free market works vs. the added complexity and costs associated with government intervention.

The same principle would apply to all goods and services. If government got out of the way, costs would go down. In California, somewhere around seventy cents for every gallon of gasoline is pure taxes. That adds up over time.

Beginning with the black-market model, the grower usually doubles as the drug dealer to end consumers. He has a cost associated with growing an amount of marijuana. In the example below, we assume the grower's cost to be $150 to produce an ounce and that he adds a 100 percent markup, resulting in a 50 percent gross margin. Remember: *(revenue – costs) / revenue = ($300 – $150) / $300 = 50 percent margin)*. From there, our black-market model assumes the pothead purchases the weed at the $300 selling price, and that's the final transaction before consumption.

Black-Market Model	
Cost of production:	$150.00
100 percent markup:	$150 + (100% × 150) = $300
Gross Margin = 50%:	(Price - Cost)/Price = (300-150)/300 = 50%
Final Price of an Ounce	$300.00

Most drug dealers don't calculate a true cost of production. Cannabis employees are off the books (or work for weed), and the profit model is simple and efficient. The supply side knows his or her operation is very profitable. The demand side is willing to pay $300 fairly often for an ounce of weed, and the velocity of selling is high as hell and consistent. People love this model. The only wrench ever thrown in the mix is if a dealer or user is caught by the police, who intervene and trample into this market. But even with the risk and life costs of incarceration, another bozo is always willing to step up and fill the void the former dealer left behind.

In a free, unregulated market, an ounce of weed is routinely broken up into smaller amounts and sold to those without access to the source grower. Then the person with access to the source grower is able to fund and repurchase additional ounces from the farm quite often. Point is, this is a thriving market, and the rate of sale—total sales dollars divided by the number of business days (or "daily sales average")—is consistent. If someone gets too old to get high or decides to progress to acid, another high school kid is waiting in the wings to start skipping class for bong-loads with buddies.

Imagine no fear of incarceration applied to this model. How cheap can you get things online shopping on Craigslist or at garage sales vs. the brick-and-mortar model burdened by government with taxes, regulations, permits, fees, and laws that ultimately punish the consumer with higher prices?

Just how big of an impact can the government's sticky paws have on the cost of a product? In the black-market model above, an ounce costs $300 to the consumer with access to a source grower, which qualifies almost any serious user for this price level. Now, let's look at the Colorado distribution model. This means switching to a model where growers and retailers are segregated, plus three government taxes for the grower, distributor, and retail store. Factoring in the added tax costs, the price soars to $691.59. Please peruse below for a value-added tax model applied to the cannabis industry (a 10 percent tax added at every level of production, distribution, and selling).

*	Legalized, Regulated Model (10 % Value Added Tax)	
G	Cost of production (1 oz. of cannabis)	$150.00
	50% markup	$150 + (.50 × 150) = $225
	Add Government: 10% Grower Tax	0.10 × $225 = $22.50
W	Wholesale purchase price	$247.50
	Wholesale adds: 50% markup	$123.75
	Wholesale selling price	$371.25
	Add government: 10% wholesale tax	$37.13
R	Final purchase price for retail	$408.38
	Retail adds: 50% markup	= .50 × 408.38 = $204.19
	Retail selling price	= $408.38 + $204.19 = $612.57
	Add government: 10% retail tax	= .10 × 612.57 = $61.26
	Add government: 2.9% state sales tax	= 0.029 × $612.57 = $17.76
	Final price of an ounce	$691.59

*G = Grower
*W = Wholesale Distributor
*R = Retailer

What are some takeaways? Well, let's break it down and disdain for government over-regulation may start to brew. How much did government collect in taxes using this VAT (Value Add Tax) model?

Taxes Collected:
Grower Taxes = $22.50
+Wholesaler Taxes = $37.13
+Retail Sales Taxes = $61.26 + $17.76

$138.65 paid in taxes out of $691.59 cash paid by end-user.

Government alone added $138.65 to the transaction above, taking home 20 percent of the $691.59 paid for an ounce of chronic. This is the reality Colorado is facing with its hyperactive market regulation and only a 10% VAT was used in the example above. Why? Because government feels the need to reap the rewards of weed legalization, just as with every market. This sparks the philosophical debate usually explored on college campuses. Is government spending the money it takes out of your pocket wisely? How much is too much? Where should government money go? Do you see nice roads and parks, or politicians with mansions on the hillside? Is there a ton of waste and bureaucracy? Does money shipped to a national capitol building three thousand miles away result in a disconnect from local needs? Is it morally wrong that someone who does not believe in abortion (due to religious beliefs) sees their tax dollars shipped to Planned Parenthood to fund free abortions? Yes, a tiny percentage of abortions may be to save a woman's life, but what about the drunk girl who had unprotected sex and didn't want to take responsibility for her actions? What is that abortion to a baby with a beating heart?

Most people won't consider the politics involved relative to taxation, but if a transaction is as simple as the two-party, $300-an-ounce black-market transaction above, no politics are involved. Now, people are going to cry, kick, and scream about the children and bullshit causes they claim to believe in. I don't buy it, and there is something to be learned about the simplicity of a black-market transaction. Get regulation, police, and laws out of the equation, and things become isolated to a mutual agreement and exchange between two parties.

Let's take it back to the old-school currency example at the beginning of this chapter. Why does it matter? It is important to think of market transactions in terms of complexity, conversion, and the ability to exchange commodities fluidly. If the market were a simple mechanism determined by two mutually agreeing parties, the costs and benefits would be weighed exclusively between two mutual participants. That decision to exchange would be based entirely on the value of the commodity to each. Think about the purity. The simplicity. This free-market transaction is almost as pure as a pair of white pants on a hot Santa Barbara chick's booty.

Then the trouble starts. We do not live in a free market, despite what is taught in the teacher-unionized education system. Every transaction is taxed. Different industries are taxed more heavily than others. As with the weed example, certain industries are taxed at multiple stages of production. The evil oil companies get vilified by the media and politicians. The banks are another sector of industry that takes a thumping. Who suffers in the end? The consumer! Even if you can't stand potheads and think they are deadbeats, there are industries out there facing the same persecution and government witch hunts. You may or may not hold those companies in high regard, but that is beside the point.

The most important thing to learn from the example above is that when government "sticks it" to a certain industry via heavy regulation and taxes, costs rise. The consumer gets screwed in the end by paying more for the commodity. This puts perspective and truth on the Barney Frank regulations (post-2008 financial crisis) in the banking industry. Government's intervention into free markets with forced redline lending in the housing industry specifically played a part leading up to the collapse. It was the banks that absorbed the blame after the collapse happened, which was a bit unfair. The Dodd-Frank Banking Reform Act almost immediately resulted in higher credit card interest rates, with banks no longer providing free checking account services. I don't need to cite that because I lived through it. The new banking capital and cash flow requirements forced banks' hands to stick it to the consumer. It wasn't as if the cash would appear out of nowhere. It had to be raised with new revenue generation (via fees) passed on to the American consumer.

This is where one must be wary of the close relationship, or disparate relationship, between big business and government versus ma and pa businesses. Big businesses have lobbyists perched up in Washington like turkey vultures. Politicians tend to be money whores. They say one thing to the general public and media, then do things that benefit their financial pockets. When people bash the stock market or finance sector, they should bash government tenfold. Let's touch on the issue of currency. We currently have a situation where the US government has a currency not backed by any commodity. Does this mean that whoever runs the Federal Reserve can print money at the pull of a lever? Yes. What, if anything, regulates how much money can be printed? Nothing, really. There are certain tides of resistance against the amount of money Ben Bernanke (former chair) or Janet Yellen (new chair of the Federal Reserve) can run through the press. For all intents and purposes, these tides of resistance have not gained much momentum and definitely not any tangible power over the Fed.

In a perfect world, the population would cry foul when government says it is going to put you, the citizen, in debt to fund its irresponsible spending behavior. Make no qualms about it: government is putting American taxpayers into severe debt with deficit spending at levels unprecedented in the history of mankind. Loans are being taken out in your name (unless you don't pay taxes). For those ignorant Americans, the US government is doing this without knowledge or consent. For those aware of the situation (aside from elites who benefit from this system), this occurs without consent. Okay, so what if we have an elected, so-called representative government? Since when did being elected mean one has carte blanche authority to take out credit cards, via printing money, in someone else's name? Do you ever remember a student body being elected in high school that decided it had authority to turn around and ring up a credit card using your social security number to host parties you didn't attend, send gifts to friends from other high schools, and generally ruin your reputation as a school entirely? That is not what government was intended to do, but exactly what government is doing. The worst part is they are doing this in the name of helping the impoverished and saving children. What a sham.

The other issue at play with the Federal Reserve indiscriminately running the money machine and discriminately distributing it into the economy is that cash is not reaching working-class Americans. It must pass through the wall of corporations in bed with government, crony institutions, and other organizations with lobby power. These are the power players in a system where government and large players team up to keep the status quo power structure in place forever. Politicians will write laws and then invest in the companies impacted by those same laws. Total conflict of interest that has led to millionaire politicians who never get booted from office. It is not a free market. When government decides to do a round of quantitative easing, the stock market soars. Real Americans' incomes do not rise. The inflation caused by an influx of dollars into the banking system, in fact, hurts average Joes and Janes. Basic supply and demand. Additional supply of dollars into the system means the value of the dollar drops. Since the ordinary citizen does not get access to the new cash supply—instead, large banks and financial institutions do—existing dollars held by Americans hold less value. Inflation sucks.

How has the dollar continued to reign supreme despite reckless government spending? If you listen to guys like Doug Casey, The Dollar Vigilante, or Peter Schiff, they obsess over inflation leading to financial collapse. By their logic, this will occur when America is no longer able to pay its debt obligations. Without delving into whether this will happen, let's explore basic concepts of economic theory, commencing with supply and demand. When you think of goods and services in a market, a scarce amount of resources limits the amount a company can supply. On the flipside, at a given price level, only certain market participants are capable of paying (or want to pay) the amount companies charge for their products. In a perfect world (with no government intervention), we would see a market equilibrium graph that looks as such:

Market equilibrium supply and demand curve

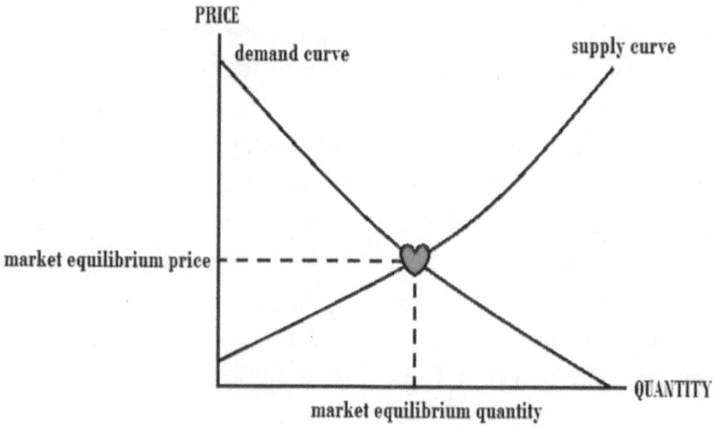

In a perfect world, a free market is based on an aggregated sum of people's individual choices. On the supply side, companies hire workers for a given price (that they are willing to work for), then produce a finished good at a set cost. Businesses mark up the cost of that good and charge a price. Customers are willing to pay for it or not. If not, the company won't be in business very long. Margins vary depending on many factors: the competitive nature of the industry, the number of units sold, and the cost to produce. Some companies even have a psychological edge over competitors based on marketing, being the first company to produce, a loyal customer base, and other factors that do not mean a better product.

What if someone took a loan out in your name and ruined your credit? What if someone swooped cash from your bank account (for bad investments) and devalued the cash you have in hand? This is all happening to American taxpayers at the hands of a swampy government. The US government has overspent to the tune of trillions of dollars. This debt is funded by yours truly, the American taxpayer. The Federal Reserve then buys this same debt via the purchase of treasury securities. The end result is debt that American taxpayers must now pay back, plus interest! Politicians have installed a mock system that degrades the value of the currency Americans use to purchase goods. Commodities purchased on the international market, such as oil and energy, have risen in price because the dollar continues to lose purchasing power due to large amounts of debt. In addition, the Federal Reserve's tactics of "quantitative easing" are hurtful as well. Quantitative easing is simply printing money out of thin air and distributing it to large financial institutions, not ordinary citizens.

What happens when you increase the supply of a good? The price goes down. Basic economics. When the Federal Reserve prints trillions of dollars, the existing value of dollars in the marketplace drops. Why? Because there are more dollars competing over the same scarce amount of goods in the market. Unfortunately, the quantitative easing dollars do not reach middle-class America. It is a system that forever enslaves the ordinary man or woman. To be blunt, you can thank politicians for gas, rent, and the cost of living being so damn expensive!

First, government intrudes into markets with tentacles of regulation that add to the cost of all transactions. You look for a decent job. Before even landing that job, you are burdened by the high cost of living and unemployment—both of which are higher than they would be in a government-free market. Government does not permit people to be paid at a price both the individual and the employer agree upon. This works to your advantage if you are unskilled. The do-nothings are overpaid. However, cutthroat competitors and valuable contributors to American business are getting screwed. Companies overpay some employees, underpay others, and do not hire those they would in a free-market scenario. This leads to the unemployment "mustache ride" shown below:

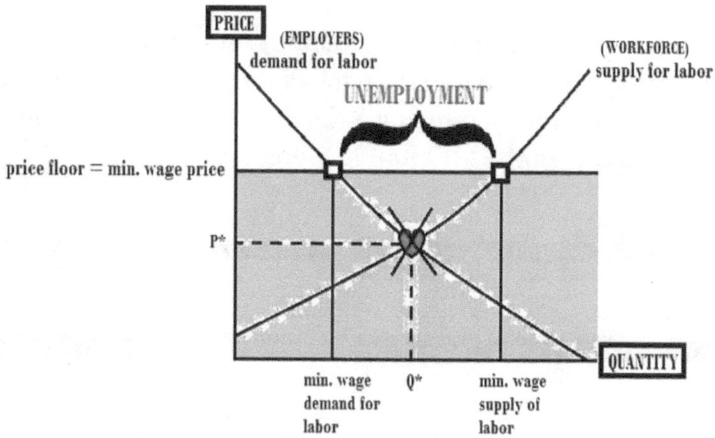

Now proposing to abolish minimum wage laws will not get you laid at a cocktail party, that's for damn sure. Minimum wage abolishment will never happen (unless the system totally collapses—back to ground zero, free-market capitalism). The sad thing nobody acknowledges is the truth: if minimum wage laws were abolished, unemployment would drop, costs to produce goods would decrease, manufacturing would return to America, and the cost of living would go down. Those are all good things, right?

Let's examine the unemployment mustache ride a bit further. Everyone loves a good flavor saver. In Economics 101, you learn the dynamics of supply and demand (with a scarce amount of goods) in the marketplace. Replace goods with labor, as in human capital, from the example above. In the graph, you see supply and demand for labor meet naturally at the equilibrium point, annotated by the heart (P* and Q* intersection). In short, the government declares that a company must pay entry-level workers more than their value truly is in a free market. When that happens, labor supplied in the marketplace at that price is greater than the aggregate sum of payroll companies are willing to pay. So what must companies do? Cut payroll in other areas, such as higher-earning mid-level management jobs. Companies cut benefits, forego research and development, degrade product quality, etc. The list goes on regarding where the squeeze comes to overpay for minimum wage. Let's demonstrate this using tables and charts to hammer it home.

True beauty rests in market equilibrium. Employees are willing to work at a price that companies are willing to pay, i.e., price equals quantity. At this level, Company XXX has a payroll consisting of 330 employees at a cost of $11,750,000 annually.

1. MARKET EQUILIBRIUM

# OF EMPLOYEES (QUANTITY)	EMPLOYEES WILLING TO WORK @ (ANNUAL)	COMPANY WILLING TO PAY (ANNUAL)	TOTAL SALARY
10	$ 150,000	$ 150,000	$ 1,500,000
20	$ 75,000	$ 75,000	$ 1,500,000
50	$ 50,000	$ 50,000	$ 2,500,000
250	$ 15,000	$ 25,000	$ 6,250,000
330			$ 11,750,000

The government comes in like the big, know-it-all asshole and declares unskilled workers are getting screwed in this setup. "They are only making $25,000 a year," says the politician. The truth is, workers are willing to work for that salary. The government then declares all workers must be paid at least $35,000 per year, regardless of job position or title. This is the easiest sell in the world because the majority of workers are in the $25,000 bracket. Those who are educated, highly skilled, long-time workers that received promotions, and made their way out of entry-level pay see no benefits from minimum wage increases. It is an easy trap to be conned into a sympathetic view regarding minimum wage hikes by government cronies. Bottom line is, minimum wage increases to $35,000 a year and total company payroll rises to $14,250,000 (if the company does nothing). The minimum wage hike for Company XXX is displayed in the table and bar chart below:

2. MINIMUM WAGE IMPLEMENTED

# OF EMPLOYEES (QUANTITY)	MINIMUM WAGE IMPLEMENTED	COMPANY MUST NOW PAY	NEW TOTAL SALARY
10	$ 150,000	$ 150,000	$ 1,500,000
20	$ 75,000	$ 75,000	$ 1,500,000
50	$ 50,000	$ 50,000	$ 2,500,000
250	$ 35,000	$ 35,000	$ 8,750,000
330			$ 14,250,000

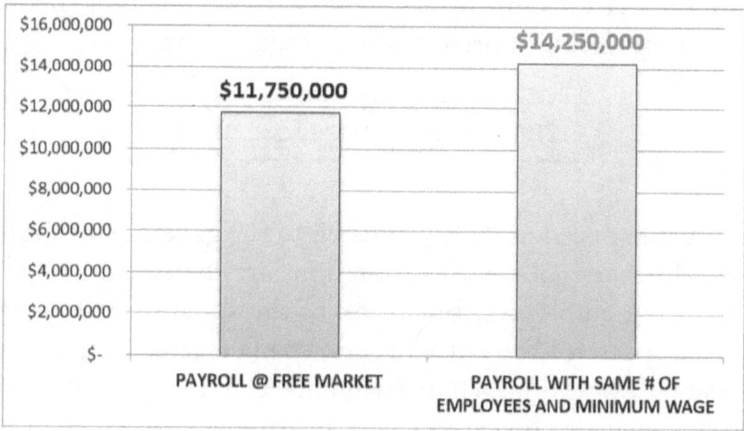

From a business perspective, government just caused your payroll to rise by 21.3 percent by adding a minimum wage hike:

Percentage Change = (New – Old)/Old
= (New Payroll – Old Payroll) / Old Payroll
= ($14,250,000 – $11,750,000) / $11,750,000
= $2,500,000 change / $11,750,000 original payroll
= 21.3%

Companies exist to earn a profit. Therefore, Company XXX has a few options to maintain its profit margins:

1. *Cut salary levels* of employees earning above minimum wage

2. *Cut number of employees*—This is how government is to blame for unemployment.
3. *Raise prices*—This is an example of how government regulation leads to inflation.
4. *Get in bed with government*—That way Company XXX can avoid paying taxes, get government subsidies, or find other creative, fascist ways to use government as an ally. Nonprofits are a shining example of this category.

In summary, Company XXX must cut $2.5 million to maintain its current profitability, pre-minimum wage increase.

COMPANY'S BUDGET FOR SALARIES	$	11,750,000
PAYROLL AFTER MIN. WAGE INCREASE	$	14,250,000
COMPANY MUST CUT:	$	(2,500,000)

What happens next? If you listen to the government's version of how the story goes, evil corporations are the culprits responsible for firing employees. But think of the situation from a company's perspective. You can't fire upper management or seasoned professionals who run each department. A company would go into a state of chaos as objectives wouldn't be defined, goals not set, and nobody with a high level of understanding would be running key business areas. Middle management workers are the ones who suffer. Their paychecks and benefits are squeezed. They become overworked and take on too many job duties and responsibilities to make up for the loss of additional workers. Below is how a company resolves this issue of having to pay all entry-level employees $35,000:

- 20 × $75,000 per year employees are eliminated = $1,500,000 in savings
- 20 × $50,000 per year employees are eliminated = $1,000,000 in savings

Now Company XXX is able to maintain its previous level of profitability, but at the expense of upward mobility for entry-level workers. Everyone loses, including minimum wage earners!

3. CONSEQUENCE OF MINIMUM WAGE LAW

	# OF EMPLOYEES (QUANTITY)	MINIMUM WAGE IMPLEMENTED	COMPANY MUST PAY (ANNUAL SALARY)	NEW TOTAL SALARY
	10	$ 150,000	$ 150,000	$ 1,500,000
MIDDLE CLASS JOB CUTS	0	~~$ 75,000~~		~~$~~
MIDDLE CLASS JOB CUTS	30	$ 50,000	$ 50,000	$ 1,500,000
	250	$ 35,000	$ 35,000	$ 8,750,000
	290			$ 11,750,000

For those who don't enjoy tables, scope the charts below. You can see a scenario where Company XXX employs 330 workers in a market equilibrium situation. This leaves healthy numbers of total workers and workers in the higher income brackets. Entry-level workers have more opportunity to rise into the $50,000, $75,000, and $150,000 jobs because there are simply more of them!

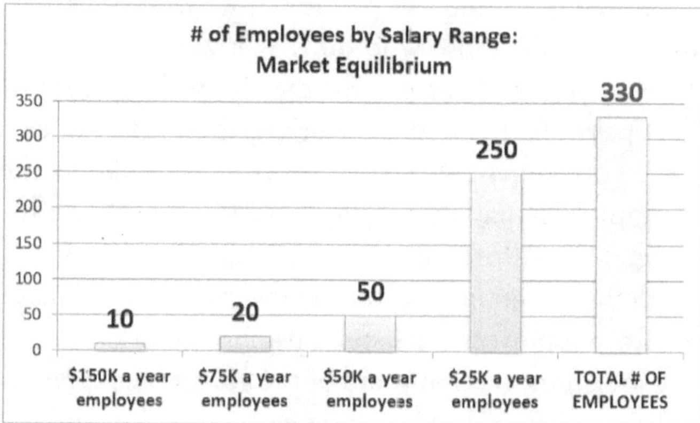

Then you look at what happens when minimum wage hits the workforce. There are very few $50,000, $75,000, and $150,000 opportunities, as displayed below. So the same number of entry-level workers are competing for a much smaller amount of high-paid positions. Opportunities for advancement and the American middle-class dream are depleted.

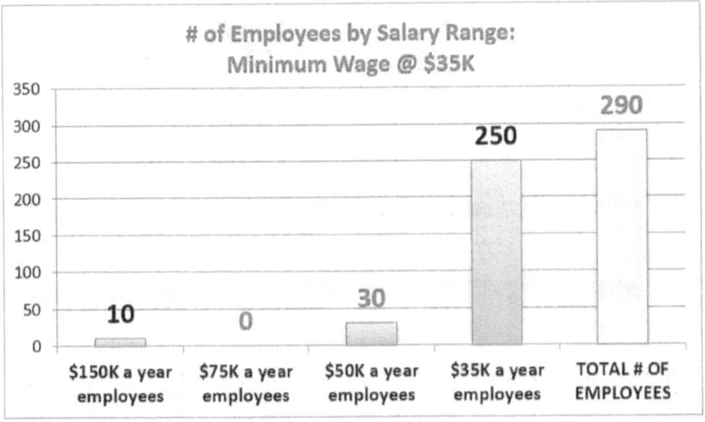

This demonstrates why middle-class Americans get squeezed like a fat chick's FUPA stuffed in a corset! Big government burdens business with heaps of decrees and regulatory costs passed on to corporations. Instead of helping, they eliminate upward mobility and middle-class living. Employees pay for those who don't work. They pay medical costs for those who don't work. They pay housing for those who don't work. They pay for the children of those who don't work. They pay welfare for those working cash jobs under the table (but tell the government they don't work). They pay for free meals and education. They pay those simply based on race or ethnic background. I read the Affordable Care Act, and it was stuffed full with billions of dollars in grants specifically for minorities to become doctors or nurses. Employees were stuck paying for all of it!

If you are on the receiving end of the government gravy train and raiding tax money from hardworking employees, you are completely okay with this setup! You justify it with no shame: your family was discriminated against (even though everyone's family has been discriminated against at some point in history), you were bullied (even though standing up to the bully is one of life's most important lessons), or you have red hair (even though redheads are said to be freaks in bed)! For fuck's sake, the list goes on. Every one of us could justify why we deserve government entitlements and preferential treatment—if we were all giant pussies! I'll save my sob story for another book, but the truth is, this system takes away from talented, go-getters and redistributes to those at the bottom. Then those at the bottom have less opportunity for upward mobility—a lose-lose outcome!

If you plan on being stagnant at the entry-level position forever, the system works well for you. You are overpaid $35,000 a year when you are worth $25,000 in free market equilibrium. If you plan to compete, move up through the ranks, and make it to mid-level management, those opportunities are no longer available for you. This results in getting stuck in the La Brea tar pits of socioeconomic mediocrity! Management opportunities and middle-class living are more difficult to come by. Job requirements become much greater as the system employs fewer managers to execute the same amount of work.

At your next cocktail party, put it out there. Give a real-life example of someone you witnessed who isn't worth $25,000 a year. Think of the $80,000 a year DMV worker. Are they worth that? Government jobs don't follow the equilibrium standard, nor do they have to cut costs for minimum wage laws such as normal businesses. They even overpay workers and offer retirement pensions non-existent in the private sector. Look at your pay stub and add up the taxes levied on all your earnings and spending. Look at the national debt and how much interest the US government must pay on that debt monthly with taxpayer dollars!

Put forth your own analysis. Tune out the news pundits. Fuck the noise that ethnicity is cause for special treatment. Turn the barrage of sob stories into the truth. American middle-class opportunities are being eliminated because of bastards adding no value to society and being overpaid for it.

Next time you hear the minimum wage is too low, tell them you think it's too high! Since you plan on being an achiever, those overpaid minimum wage workers are limiting opportunities. Make note of every purchase and how your dollar doesn't go as far because company earnings, your earnings, and personal spending are overtaxed like a dirty wench! Who knows, some girl at a cocktail party may just get riled up enough to give you a good old-fashioned.

Chapter 5

COLD, HARD REPORTING FACTS

WE'RE GROWING, AND WE'RE GROWING FAST. WE are a high-growth company. Everything is growing. Our balls is hot from growing so fast! Our company and customers are better than you, and we know it! While owners & executives are obsessed with growth, just remember the reason. Most companies payout their entire profits to owners (or shareholders) and barely make payroll month to month, requiring a line of credit in the event cash gets tight. So while you may believe that a company growing exponentially is going to be some huge benefit for you (executives are always preaching this BS), staff will continue to be paid based on roles & responsibilities. Yes, hope your company is financially profitable, work towards a promotion, but also realize the growth obsession is hogwash. You aren't going to become a millionaire working for a company without being an owner or significant shareholder. I pity us fools!

Growth, growth, growth

Some companies experiencing growth exaggerate (or believe) they are growing above and beyond what numbers tell. Many companies don't run proper reports to truly gauge growth. They do not analyze where growth is coming from. A company could be around for twenty years but still not measure itself against relative historical data because it believes every month is a high-growth month compared to the previous one. "Our company and its products aren't seasonal!" Yeah, but weather, human beings, and business cycles are! This chapter will explore fundamental concepts of reporting and leveraging different comparisons to understand a company's full picture relative to business performance.

Quantitative analysis brings about a set of ethical issues that must be acknowledged from the start. Working in the profession of data analytics, having studied countless analyses in the news and academia, it is safe to say numbers are easily manipulated to promote a predetermined theory or agenda. You can focus on certain aspects of a study, look only at certain members of a study, exclude certain variables, look at specific metrics while ignoring others, utilize or ignore anomalies, and employ various tactics that will allow you to paint a preconceived picture on whatever the topic may be. Your population (a statistics term) can be skewed to favor your study. In other words, some amateur analyst may start with a hypothesis in their head and go seek quantitative analysis to prove it instead of taking an objective approach.

Other times, incompetence and carelessness lead to improper conclusions. For example, the analyst could have ignored statistical significance, not properly scrubbed the data, or only focused on a certain set of factors without looking at underlying data that explains results more accurately. In the news, media, and academia, most of the inaccuracies in quantitative analysis are derived from analysts with politically loaded agendas. In business, improper analysis is usually a result of carelessness on the part of the analyst, who is either crunched for time or gets stuck in the world of numbers without taking a step back to contemplate external factors. His or her analysis may also be driven by an executive who wants to hear what they want to hear, not the truth.

The theme of this chapter is structured reporting and the potential pitfalls one encounters when not utilizing multiple modes of comparison. One cannot simply compare to an arbitrary time frame.

As stated at the beginning of the chapter, you can't be that douche bag boasting your company is immune from seasonality and destined for infinite growth. If you only compare sales to the previous day's sales, it is shortsighted and dangerous. Companies do that and end up on a roller coaster ride from hell. It creates a constant panic environment. Sales are low today—knee-jerk reaction time! Halt purchases from COGS suppliers! Discount the website! Fire drill time! Conversely, on a peak sales day, the crisis turns to hysteria, and it is catch-up time. Time to over-purchase! Never let the highs get too high or the lows too low. Company performance isn't something that should hinge on a single day. Any sales day, week, month, quarter, or season can be impacted by one of the following depending on the nature of a company:

- Mondays are always bigger sales days than the rest of the week because web orders from the weekend are processed on this day.
- Pre-Thanksgiving could be the biggest sales period for a company selling turkeys. If selling gift wrapping, then December (pre-Christmas) is when peak season occurs. Peak selling seasons traditionally tend to be during the holidays, but this may not be true for a company selling sunscreen or European banana hammock speedos. The key is to know your business cycles well and the underlying reasons for them. Why is the day after Thanksgiving called Black Friday? As mentioned previously (not to be a repeat radio ad), it's because that's the first day of the year when companies are said to get out of the red & achieve profitability from the seasonal spike in sales.
- A storm or other seasonal weather event may impact your targeted geographical area. This can happen one year and not the next. If you are unaware of external factors and events, you may make erroneous decisions based on incorrect assumptions.
- The overall health of the economy is an omnipresent factor that can turn winds quickly (and severely), impacting a company's financial performance. Our unfriendly

Feds may stop pumping billions of dollars in paper to the banking system (that gets disbursed to America's largest corporations) or make moves to stop buying the US government's own debt via treasury securities. Either of these events would lead to a deflation in the price of the big companies' stock prices, which thrive on access to cheap paper, and impact the state of global markets. While this would be a natural market correction, nobody in the world likes reality, especially fascist governments in bed with large corporations that have benefited from this setup for so long. The retail investors in the stock market (ordinary investors lacking much expertise) pull cash out, causing pandemonium in global financial markets. This would have a direct impact on most companies, regardless of size.

- Economic indicators, economic indicators! How are American salaries looking compared to the previous year? What manipulated unemployment numbers did the government release this month? How are average home prices? How about earnings on key companies across the business world spectrum? Last (and of critical importance), how is that price at the pump looking? While green Nazis proclaim Americans can use bicycles (and anal-poking unicycles) to make the world go 'round, every business is impacted by energy prices. Know how key economic indicators correlate with your industry specifically. Keep a close eye on them. Who knows, there may be some indicators that signal huge growth or downturns before they hit. Run correlation coefficients and see what you come up with.
- There could be an orange famine in Florida due to Shnookie infesting the water lines with booty juice. While this wouldn't impact all companies, if you are a smoothie maker, oranges may be one of your key ingredients, and this event would cause you to brace for price increases from your suppliers.

The point to be made here is that in business, all factors must be considered: internal, external, seasonality, the economy, complementary industries and products, and multiple time frames for relative comparison. Oftentimes, a boss will be inundated with what is going on internally with the company, so much so that he or she is blinded to the big picture. Other times, the douche bag (or vag) in charge will have preconceived notions of what the numbers should be and refuse to accept the truth of quantitative analysis when presented.

For example, the president of Company XXX may come to the analyst to determine how many individual parrots have been fed the company's miraculous birdfeed that enables the feathered beings to speak in multiple languages (including birds of the nonspeaking kind). This would be an easy task if the company had statistics on how many birds reside in each client's household. However, the only information available in the systems is ordering history on individual human purchasers. Damn birds don't call and place orders! The analyst tactfully goes down the road of determining how many birds likely reside in each customer's home who placed an order using empirical data.

1. The analyst reviews all knowns:
    a. Recommended serving size based on bird weight.
    b. Total cost per shipped container of birdfeed and the different sizes available to customers.
    c. Data on known single bird owners and detailed historical purchasing patterns.
    d. Different types of birds fed the miracle supplement and average weights.
    e. Distribution of pet bird types in homes kept as pets.
2. The analyst determines how to project the total number of birds that have been fed miracle feed over the past year:
    a. Extracts ordering history by individual customer accounts.
    b. Filters sales for only the miraculous birdfeed and omits birdcage accessories.

c. Plugs in average weight of birds based on household distribution for average bird size.
d. Analyzes bulk data on individual clients with only single birds to determine compliance and adherence to recommended serving sizes, *i.e., are clients feeding daily the exact amount as recommended, or do they miss a day here and there?*
e. Based on single bird clients, analyst projects how many birds are likely to be in each household, based on the total dollar spent on feed converted to total servings sent to each house within a given timeframe.
f. All customers who placed single orders of small container sizes are filled in as single bird owners.
g. All customers who placed large container sizes are filled in as multiple bird owners, with number of birds determined using ordering patters of multiple-time purchasing clients who ordered that sized container and likely number of birds owned in those homes.
h. Data is aggregated and summarized based on most likely case given historical averages along with a high and low based on minimum and maximum compliance ranges.
i. After summary, analyst spot-checks results on total birds fed vs. number of clients who placed orders in system during given timeframe. Quant analysis determined the table per below.

	AVERAGE	RANGE: MIN	RANGE: MAX	
# of birds	100,000	85,000	125,000	
# of clients in system	80,000	80,000	80,000	<==CONSTANT, KNOWN IN SYSTEM
avg. # of birds per household	1.25	1.06	1.56	

The analyst has gone through all the proper steps, conversions, plugged in as much historical data as possible. They have spot-checked results for reasonability. If the results had shown average number of birds per household to be ten, then it would go against commonsense and red flag a mistake along some point in the quantitative analysis. Without going through every step of the calculation, for time's sake, a few things are to be noted. Based on historical ordering patterns of clients with single birds and compliance, the average is the most likely case scenario using empirical data from past clients. The minimum and maximum are determined from the outliers of the data set, those clients who were either way out of compliance or adhered 100 percent to compliance (analyzed in unison with maximum and minimum bird weights). The main point here is the analyst has performed a thorough analysis, using the best conversion and historical ordering data available in the systems. In their summary, the analyst walks Captain CEO through the steps of analysis used at each stage and presents the most likely scenario of 100,000 birds being fed the talking supplement in the past year. The results show a minimum and maximum range from 85,000 to 125,000. The steps were logical. A range was determined based on extreme scenarios being actuals. The analyst answered the question being asked, using solid quantitative analysis.

Big business egos may have a preconceived result in their minds—a number they believe to be true. In the case of government unemployment statistics, the analyst may go in with a number he is expected to hit. In other unethical scenarios, an analyst may walk in with a point they are trying to make or a hypothesis to prove. In the case of the talking birdfeed, the CEO may not be quantitatively gifted (*since many at the top of the corporate ladder achieved their position via nepotism or worked their way up through politics and soft communication skills rather than hard, numerical-analytical capabilities*). They may also have a foregone conclusion that the number of birds fed is half a million based on a deranged calculation using bogus math. When the analyst presents the range of 85,000 to 125,000, with one hundred thousand as the most likely case scenario, the CEO simply ignores it. They don't like the truth in numbers and will continue to present half a million birds fed annually as the spoken gospel of company lore.

This is when ego and emotions can blind companies to the truth of mathematical calculations. The CEO attempts to rationalize his miscalculation: "We are an X-million-dollar-a-year company. If we are doing X dollars a day, we have to feed at least a half million birds!" What is the analyst to do at this slap in the face to the history of mathematics? Should they soil their pants and walk off the job? That's one way to handle it. Should they slap their prideful boss in the face and yell, "Homey don't play that!" No, in corporate America, if you don't own the company or aren't Captain CEO, a tactful response is usually the best way to go. Here are a few responses to consider:

- "You know, I think you're right. I always suspected Bill Gates created Excel to return faulty calculations and aggregations!"
- "Let me recheck my assumptions. I think we can manipulate the data to hit your target number!"
- "I'll take your word over my own any day. Half a million birds it is!"
- Look very seriously into your CEO's eyes, squint as if intently thinking, nod your head in approval, and confirm his hunch by speaking slowly and methodically, "Absolutely!"
- "You know, what household doesn't have six and a quarter birds?"

	CEO says:
Number of birds	500,000
Number of clients in system	80,000
avg. number of birds per household	6.25

- Smile, tuck your tail between your legs, and think to yourself, *I need a job, and this ain't a battlefield I'm willing to die on.* Don't be Jesus sacrificing yourself on the cross over ego.

It is always good to be prepared in the business world, and life in general, for people to not believe the truth when you speak it. In fact, if you gravitate more toward quantitative analysis, many will feel insecure or offended when you present a report using numbers. For whatever reason, math has been stigmatized in American society as this big asshole juggernaut that everyone should fear. Without getting too much into the whys, my personal theory blames a few actors in the equation. First, as one grows older, you realize that some high school teachers are actually huge pieces of shit. That's right. They went into teaching because they were lazy, wanted summers off, had big egos easily inflated around fifteen-year-olds, and were generally incapable of excelling in the competitive environment of business. That's not to say all, as there are obviously great teachers out there who do a noble job, work their tails off, and perform God's work in the classroom by being an inspiration for the next generation. However, high school teachers aren't always going to inspire the same way a kid would be by discovering a passion on their own. Many educators destroy far more kids' confidence levels and futures than empower them.

The second aspect of society I blame for the lack of mathematical savvy (and widespread fear of quant anything) is the American system of education. This albatross is burdened down by government bureaucracy and increasingly regulated from the far-off land of Oz, Washington, DC. Education is an indoctrination tool; ask Castro, Stalin, Lenin, Hitler, Mao, or any Commie dictator from history. If schools were competing against one another, maintaining local identity, harnessing unique cultural differences and identity, and channeling innovative ways to improve education (without being held to Washington's one-size-fits-all, outdated standards), we might find unique ways to enhance the educational model for math and sciences. If I was personally involved in high school curriculum for math and sciences, I would immediately launch fundamental business finance and applied mathematics programs. Get kids to understand personal finance, corporate financial statements, and what the stock market actually is, and fewer people would be making irresponsible monetary decisions. If you implemented a program with kids understanding how Euclidean geometry developed and the underlying calculations used to determine distances between Earth and its universal counterparts, kids might actually get fascinated with math and the sciences. Instead, most high school students are face-fucked with a few equations unenticing to simpleton minds, and then the masses forever fear numbers. Just some food for thought as politicians, complain, then try to implement stupid testing systems. Teachers prepare kids for bubble exams that do nothing for long-term capabilities.

Proper analysis can amount to overkill on any subject matter if one allows it to happen. You can slice, dice, and look at data until the world ends and still not cover all your bases. Questions are a continuum from the non-quant crowd, because they do not understand that math yields a correct (or incorrect) result. As a professional analyst, the onus is on you to determine relevant ways to present information and cover applicable points depending on the analysis being concocted.

Put your hands down the panties, pet some beaver, and discover ways an analysis can be presented to open one's mind to endless possibilities. Traditional reporting will focus on set timeframes for comparison, such as month-end snapshots. To gauge overall company performance, there are benefits to traditional monthly, quarterly, and annual reporting. First, publicly traded companies are required by law to file quarterly and annual reports with the Securities Exchange Commission using GAAP (generally accepted accounting practices) for compliance. Traditional reports use year-over-year (YOY) comparison, meaning you compare the given timeframe to the previous year, same timeframe, and then determine a percentage and dollar increase. An easy way to think of YOY percentage growth comparison is to calculate:

Percent Change = (New – Old) / Old
March 2014: $5,500,000 in sales
March 2013: $5,250,000 in sales
Step 1: Percent Change = ($5,500,000 - $5,250,000) / $5,250,000
Step 2: Percent Change = $250,000 / $5,250,000
Step 3: Percent Change = 0.047619047
Step 4: Slide the decimal over two places ➔ 0.047619047 = 4.76 percent

Any sort of percent change should be thought of in these terms. Always pay heed to parentheses while writing Excel calculations, or your order of operations is flawed. If you have multiple segments of your business, one cannot become tied to percentage growth alone. It is vital to gauge dollar growth—for instance, the $250,000 in the simple example above. Why is that? Well, you may have a tiny segment of the business that is growing at 60 percent, which may lead to people hooting and hollering, but in reality, 60 percent growth might represent an insignificant dollar amount.

Perhaps that 60 percent growth (in dollar terms) was minuscule and caused by a one-time, one-off purchase. Let's force the math equation to display how 60 percent growth for a small business segment can actually be one-tenth the size of 4.76 percent growth.

60 percent growth of a company's revenue x = 10% × $250,000
60 percent growth of a company's revenue x = only $25,000
60 percent x = $25,000
0.6x=$25,000
X=25,000/0.6
Company Revenue X=$41,666.67
vs.
4.76 percent growth of a company's revenue X = $250,000
4.76 percent X=$250,000
0.0476X=$250,000
X=250,000/0.0476
Company X Revenue=$5,252,100.84

So if you have a company or business segment that brings in $41,666.67 of revenue, 60 percent growth amounts to only $25,000, while 4.76 percent growth for a $5.25 million company equates to roughly $250,000 (10x growth dollars) in the examples above. Now which company has the bigger advantage? Would you prefer 60 percent growth or 4.76 percent growth? Well, it depends on the size of the business, you clever strategist, you. Don't lose sight of that! This is why it is important never to tie yourself too closely to a single metric, such as percentage growth.

Consider dollar growth, growth in daily averages, growth of each business sector relative to the size of the business, different comparison periods, and internal and external events not conveyed in a numerical report or chart. In other words, be a true analyst. Keep your eyes wide open and consider different perspectives that lead to additional insights.

If you are in government, you can just flat-out lie. Yes, you heard that correctly. If you work in government statistics, it is normal (and acceptable) to tell completely inaccurate stories, revise stories at a later time, and release metrics that misguide the public entirely. Don't believe me? Let's take a look at a Yahoo Finance article on 2014 GDP growth:

> *The economy grew at an annual rate of 4% in the second quarter according to the Bureau of Economic Analysis. The government also revised its GDP reading for the first quarter higher, from negative 2.9% to negative 2.1%, but revised 2011–2013 growth lower, from 2.2% to 2%. (http://finance.yahoo.com/news/q2-is-the-best-economic-growth-we-ll-have-all-year--peter-schiff-123736174.html)*

If you smell bullshit in the quote above, you aren't the only one. Above is a huge pile of lies and dick cheese, fromunda. Imagine if you could concoct this scheme in private business. Your company would be omni-successful upon financials being released. Essentially, government is inflating—*blatantly lying* about—results at time they occur and simultaneously downward revising *historical lies*, so baseline is smaller to measure against, making current results more successful in today's news headlines. It's the double whammy! How does government get away with propaganda on such a massive scale? Thank mainstream media being completely, shamelessly, and mindlessly in on the scam. Without them giving each other hand jobs around the clock, this would be a highly contentious issue.

Let's have a look-see in tabular format. In reality below, we have two columns simultaneously running: Column 1 (the government bed of lies or results they put forward and later revise) and Column 2 (actual results).

	1. Government Lies	2. Actual Results
2012	$100,000,000	$85,000,000
2013	$120,000,000	$90,000,000
2014	$125,000,000	$100,000,000

Back in the golden days, sales results were finalized and published accurately the first time around. In fact, laws apply to corporations that mandate a company must disclose in a timely manner any material information to its shareholders. When a company releases its annual earnings report, if something is inaccurate or uncertain, it would have to be disclosed in a very clear manner. The reporting of fallacious numbers (known to be revised next year) would be a *very* material point requiring full disclosure. That is unless you are the government of the United States of Socialist America (USSA). Then the progression goes a little something like this:

1. Actual Results and Growth Figures:

	Actual Results	Actual Growth
2012	$85,000,000	Base Year
2013	$90,000,000	6 percent
2014	$100,000,000	11 percent

2. Government inflates current year and compares to revised (downward) actual results from prior year.

	Lies	Actual	Announced Growth in News
2012	$ 100,000,000 →	$ 85,000,000	BASE YEAR
2013	$ 120,000,000 →	$ 90,000,000	41 percent

2014	$ 125,000,000	$ 100,000,000	39 percent

This is the double whammy effect! You get the boost of lying about current year results, plus an additional boost of revising previous year (baseline) downward. In 2013, you show 41 percent growth (vs. 6 percent actual) by calculating:

Government report for news headlines on fake growth:

- ➔ (current year's lies – last year's actual) / (last year's actual)
- ➔ (120,000,000 – 85,000,000)/85,000,000
- ➔ 41 percent growth!

Instead of being honest and calculating:

- ⇨ (current year's actual – previous year's actual) / previous year's actual
- ⇨ (90,000,000 - 85,000,000) / 85,000,000
- ⇨ 6 percent growth.

This is how the government constantly props up the economy with bogus GDP growth numbers (released for current news cycles). They compare current false, unverified numbers (lies) to the baseline period's actual results. The baseline period (previous year) was revised downward (low-key) at some point to avoid making a stir. The end result is that the government is able to release twofold inflated growth numbers with no accountability.

As one begins to chart a life path of constant scrutiny, hopefully, tales from this chapter open minds to the depths of analysis and reasoning required for comprehensive and infallible conclusions. If you have not taken statistics, it will be difficult to fully explain anomalies, confirm to one's boss whether or not a sample size is large enough, explain standard deviation and what it means, and fully withstand the barrage of inquiry from your dickhead (or vag-face) boss who does not comprehend elementary math. Be prepared for them to whip out completely random, unrelated events to poke holes in your analytical work. Smile, be happy, and think of how miserable their gold-digging mate at home must be having to sleep with them sometimes.

Explore your options:

1. Understand and be able to explain statistics when called upon while viewing and analyzing the most relevant metrics for each given situation after a thorough data scrub that eliminates irrelevant records.
2. Go down the rabbit hole of eternal analysis to such a great level of detail that you put forth every piece of raw data and end up with little or no actionable conclusions.
3. Work for the government and lie your ass off!

Chapter 6

MATH IS FUN, KIDS, MMKAY!

Everyone is fearful of math, and for good reason. Most cannot conceptualize advanced mathematical concepts (all grounded in logic) and, as a result, don't have a handle on the ability to act rationally. The two go hand in hand. Throw emotions into the mix, and you get sheeple out there acting like a bunch of jackasses when the "M" word is used at all. The thing with math is that many people avoid becoming functional at it because they were embarrassed growing up in an education system that constantly reinforced their self-doubt and ineptitude at crunching numbers. American society has a group of disenfranchised people whose fear of math has dumbed down humanity, making it acceptable to openly claim, "I hate math." Math probably hates you too (and so do I), jk! I do like rational people and thoughts. I love the order of math. I love the certainty. It answers all questions, doesn't lie, and is always there for me as a beautiful backdrop to paint pictures grounded in truth. Math is like the perfect girlfriend that doesn't exist!

To be successful operating in business, an understanding of how math works and the ability to perform fundamental analysis are required. So for all the sales and marketing people who prefer a conversation about how you feel, close this book and go set up a

VIP booth; totally kidding. The good news is you don't need to be good at math to be functional at math. Nobody is going to test you on derivatives, differential equations, statistical analysis, standard deviations, multiple regression, infinitesimal calculus, or binomial theorem. If you are hesitant reading this chapter, let's drop our balls on the face of perspective.

In layman's terms, math has a progression of difficulty. Each progressive step is used to solve specific problems. Let's walk through the progressions and be specific as to what is required for business-math acumen. I will also include some tricks and tips to help you become, at the very least, aware of areas where you need to improve. Let's begin with level-one mathematics. Level-one mathematics is what most people learn as kids: addition, subtraction, multiplication, and division. Now, I will start by saying that this layer of math is that which people operate under and believe signifies someone being "good at math," both truthfully and erroneously. Let me explain. Being someone who has worked using math my entire life, loves math, has an MBA in finance, and received an A in my quantitative analysis class for my master's program (which is all statistics), I can say that I am very comfortable with any level of math described in this chapter. It is annoying to me that a reputation for being "good at math" among mainstream society is confined to level-one operators who do not understand the full mathematical spectrum. Dealing with level-one, rudimentary math operators annoys me.

In meetings or social situations, certain people blurt out random level-one math issues and expect to be validated through verbal math. Or they may challenge a math-minded individual for an answer off the top of one's head. Math is not sales and marketing. It is not talking. Math is problem solving with a paper trail to vouch for it. If you want to be a math person, put pencil to paper, learn Excel, perform analysis, learn the order of operations, and solve problems on a deeper level than shouting, "So what does that equal? Where's our math guy?" Doing that makes for an awkward social setting, unnecessarily puts people on the spot, and runs counter to the history of mathematics.

Archimedes, the great Greek mathematician, was said to have been murdered during the siege of Syracuse while solving mathematical problems in the sand (circa 212 BC). While the Roman Republic army was given orders not to harm him, a soldier came in, mistook him for a lunatic, shouted intrusive orders, didn't listen to his response, and killed one of antiquity's greatest math minds. His famous last words were translated to, "Don't disturb my circles," in reference to the complex diagrams he had depicted. The moral of the story is, true math is complex to the point that it shouldn't be shouted out in a room but revered, verified on paper, and demonstrated to be accurate.

Revere math, respect it, and understand its capabilities. Most everything we know about outer space? Yeah, math solved it. Enjoy driving around in your stupid Prius? Math was involved at every stage of the production line. Aspire to join the mile-high club? As you let out screams of ecstasy, thank the math gods for the ability to be at that altitude. Math is at the center of all things in the universe and all of mankind's technological advancements. To come into an office and proclaim, "I hate math" makes you sound like a total ignoramus. If you had a bad experience in elementary and high school with incompetent teachers, get over it and embrace the power of math in the workplace.

If you are competent or gifted in math, then beware as situations arise when one is challenged by dumbass sheeple who don't understand math, yet poke and pry when you present quantitative analysis. Part of being quantitatively gifted is being able to make the complex seemingly easy. Growing up, whenever I would find unconventional solutions not being taught in the classroom to math problems, teachers would note, "That is an engineer's mind" at work. This isn't to boast of myself or try to sound cool. It is to make the point that math is about going from the complex to clarity, from a problem to a solution, the unknown to the known, and making order out of chaos. The earliest stages of math were developed using axioms, which are statements or lines of reasoning that are so well thought out and demonstrable that you cannot deny their truth. While you may understand mathematical solutions in terms of being an axiom of undeniable truth, others may not. Many humans have unconventional, unstructured minds that do not live within the confines of mathematical reasoning. Unless you are at the CEO level, your quantitative solution will not be the final verdict in the workplace. In fact, a CEO who lacks a math brain will try to drag a definitive solution into the world of chaos and unstructured mumbo jumbo. That is where they reside, unable to follow lines of reasoning leading to definitive solutions. Always stick to your fundamentals, walk tall through the land of chaos, reverse every logical step, dissect every angle, and rationalize your mathematical work so that no rock is left unturned.

Think of modern, abstract artists sitting around discussing a masterpiece they created. Imagine the words they use to describe it and how their thoughts progress. The explanations conjure up images: a big circle of pooh culminating in a mushy pile of undefined form. Compare that to a billion-dollar company's CFO releasing a quarterly earnings report. Gross revenue, cost of goods sold, profit margins, net earnings, earnings before taxes, year-over-year growth, and year-to-date growth: the results are orderly, much like a progression of bullet points. Now both are valuable in their own ways. In business, you need both the circle-of-pooh thinkers and the hard-lined, square thinkers. If you manage to be both, you will do well. As in the cartoon-character-employees chapter, assess which kind of thinker you are and be cognizant of it. When you talk, do your thoughts go on for days and the room falls asleep? Or do your points seem so sharp and terse that people who get emotional tingles in meetings are offended?

Now comes the good news. In order to be business-math savvy, one does not need a master's degree in engineering, math, finance, statistics, or economics. With the proper tools, most simpletons can analyze business from a sales, marketing, operations, or any departmental perspective. The goal isn't for you to become CFO, but to go into a meeting with the CFO and not look like a complete jackass. As with most skills, there are levels of mathematical learning. From my perspective, they run from levels I through IV. Most business math operates in levels I or II, depending on the complexity of the situation. If one operates in statistics, analytics, engineering, computer science, algorithms, or other high-level technical positions, business math levels III and IV are required. What are the IV levels of math used as applied to business? While these may be arbitrary definitions I'm pulling from my ass, they are categories based on empirical truths from years of experience. Think of this as diagnosing someone with bipolar disease using the DSM-V booklet; someone built those categories and checklists that make the world consider you bipolar or not. So here go the raw, girthy, and cut levels of mathematical concepts.

Level 1

This is the mathematics you learn in elementary school: addition, subtraction, multiplication, and division. Anyone with half a brain can do this shit at a functional level. Shit, most three-year-olds can add and subtract. There are varying degrees of level I mathematics. Maybe you lost your ability to perform long division or multiplication of ten-digit numbers. Okay, no big deal (although quite embarrassing). Just don't tell a damn soul in the office—get a calculator and learn how to use Excel.

Paramount to all levels of business math is the ability to transform *word* problems into *mathematical* problems and work out a solution. No need to quickly multiply three-digit numbers in your head or blurt an answer when someone asks what 347 × 245 is equal to in a meeting. However, simple tricks and tips will allow you to open up your level-one math game and appear as someone quantitatively functional. Here we go:

- Understand your strengths and weaknesses. If you have a tough time adding numbers in your head, have pen and paper available and quickly jot down numbers and run the arithmetic on paper or set the tone and bring a calculator to meetings. Learn how to use that *sonuvabitch*. Get your fingers acquainted with her keys and quickly manipulate them for the quickest path to an answer. Practice ten key at home or on your desk computer. It is sort of like the work that goes in to sexual performance—find the clit, massage her, taste her, and find out her rhythm and what makes her climax.

- When multiplying, for sake of estimates, think in tens and sliding that decimal place over.

  Don't be scared to round. For example, if you were going to multiply 35 × 9, round up to 35 × 10. Do the same for 35 × 100 × 1,000 × 10,000, and so on per below.
  - 35 × 10 ➔ 35 + one zero ➔ 350, mofo.
  - 35 × 100 ➔ 35 + two zeros ➔ 3,500, biatch.
    - For multiplying by 100s, you can also just say "35 hundred," so essentially it solves itself. Limit here is two-digit numbers × 100 because saying a 3-digit number or greater (i.e., "456 hundred") doesn't hold.
  - 35 × 1,000 ➔ 35 + Three Zeros ➔35,000, homey.
    - For multiplying by 1,000, you can say "35 thousand" and the multiplication solves itself. Limit here is multiplying a three-digit number by 1,000 because four digits won't allow for the straight reading trick of "number-thousand." For example, 4,567 is a four-digit number and breaks the trick. Nobody says "4,567 thousand."
  - 35 × 10,000 ➔ *35 + Four zeros* ➔ 350,000, douche.

Are we noticing a pattern above? Just add the zeros to the number you are multiplying by 10. How many zeros in 35 × 100,000?

Just write 35 + the five zeros after the one in 100,000:

➔ 35 + 00,000
➔ 3,500,000
➔ 3.5 million

Operating in multiples of ten will usually get you in the ballpark for most rough estimates. It will also demonstrate intelligence in group settings when things don't need to be exact, and you may not have access to a calculator. You can be the human calculator instead. Just don't be a human centipede because that whole ATM stuff is pretty foul.

The great thing about thinking in tens is that you can start with ten to get in the ballpark and then use that number to add on an additional estimate. Let's say someone wants to know how much revenue the company will do over the next year is the daily average sales is 34,000. So 34,000 × 365 days. Do you want to chicken scratch that down real quick for an exact number? You can if you have access to paper. However, if someone expects a ballpark answer now, you can think of it like this:

Actual: 34,000 × 365
Think Instead: 34,000 × 100 × 3.65 times

➔ Start with 34,000 × 100
➔ 3,400,000
➔ So $3,400,000 × 3.65

Let's substitute 3.5 for 3.65 to and 3.4 for 3,400,000 to make thinking in your head more simple.

New equation: 3.4 × 3.5
➔ 3.4 + 3.4 + 3.4 + 1/2 (of 3.4)

The head count sounds something like "3, 6, 9, plus 0.4 × 3 = 1.2, added to 9…so 10.2…plus half of 3.4. So add another 1.7. 10 + almost 2. Okay, around 12 million."

If you have a calculator, the actual answer is $12,410,000. Breaking the multiplication down can get you very close, depending on your mental arithmetic skills and how exact you are trying to be. By simplifying, you can still arrive at a ballpark answer.

Let's be as simple as can be.
$34,000 × 365 days

So 34,000 × 100 = add two zeros to 34,000… + 00 ➔ $3.4 million

Instead of $3,400,000 × 3.65 (*since we already multiplied by 100*)

Think:

3.4 × 3.65

Let's round 3.4 down and 3.65 up.

So $3 × 4 = $12. Since our previous step, the $3.4 was million, our answer is $12 million.

Thus, we get the same answer by rounding and dropping decimals as we did trying to stick religiously to the original equation. You just have to remember which way you round to know if you are over or under. If you round both numbers up, you will be over. If you round both numbers down, you will be under. By how much always depends on how large or small the numbers are. Any time you are close to five, add half if possible. The use of rounding and then stating over or under demonstrates quick arithmetic ability. Then if you need a real check, punch the keys into the calculator and see how boss you really are. Math, as is with anything in life, requires practice to perfect. My first time I lost my virginity, it lasted maybe thirty seconds. It may have been the best thirty seconds of her life, but I've improved since (although may have regressions here and there).

Other things you need to know for level-one ability include fractions, decimals, conversions, and comparisons. This isn't tough at all. If you remember some common fractions and their decimal and percent equivalents, you will be able to conceptualize and communicate numbers to fellow team members.

You should know the following inside and out (all numbers rounded to two decimal places):

1/4 = 0.25 = 25% = 25/100 = 250/1,000…and so on.

1/3 = 0.33 = 33.33% = 33.33/100 = 333.33/1,000

1/2 = 0.50 = 50% = Half of anything, and if you don't get that, then stick to welfare, kid!

2/3 = 0.66666666666666666666 = the devil's number = 66.67% when rounded two decimal places.

3/4 = 0.75 = 75%

And of course, any number with 10 as the denominator:

1/10 = 0.10 = 10%
2.5/10 = 0.25 = 25%
3.3/10 = 0.33 = 33%
6.99/10 = 0.699 = 69.9%
7.37/10 = 0.737 = 73.7%

Basic, basic stuff, people! You need to have these tools at your mind's disposal for quick reference. Be able to quickly compare fractions between numbers for comparison. For example, say you had 5 out of 16 respondents on a survey. What is the percentage response? Well, 4 out of 16 = 4/16 = 1/4 = 25%, so you can estimate 5/16 to be somewhere around 30% (*5/16 is actually = 31.25%, but you wouldn't be expected to recall that off the top of your head).*

Let's experience a real world example. You are trolling for pussy at the local watering hole. Your goal is to try and find a slut to take home and smash so hard the neighbors think your headboard is hammering a hole through the wall. You decide to implement data tracking and tally up your attempts, base hits, phone numbers, and finally *sex-ca-pades* that actualize. Here are your stats. Over the course of a month, you hit up the bar on Thursday, Friday, or Saturday nights. You make it a goal to approach the five cutest girls you see and give them your best line. In one month, you approach sixty girls (five girls per night times three nights per week times four weeks in a month). Of those, you get six phone numbers, blowjobs from three fat chicks, and plow one hot girl. How does your scorecard look by estimating?

- Phone Numbers: 6 / 60 ➔ divide numerator and denominator by 6➔ reduced to 1 / 10 ➔ 10%. Not bad work.

- Blowjobs: 3 / 60 ➔ divide by highest common denominator (3) ➔ reduced to 1 / 20 ➔ divide by 2 to get to 10 ➔ 0.5 / 10 ➔ 5%.
- Plow Ratio: 1 / 60 ➔ 1 out of 50 would be = 2 out of 100 = 2%. You're below that, but 1 out of 60 is greater than 1 out of 100 (1%). So logically, you're batting somewhere between a 1–2% plow ratio. Actual number is 1.67% so the estimation logic was sufficient. And you got your little willy wet!

Think real world problems or issues and turn them into mathematical logic with estimations. Practice makes pussies wet!

PEMDAS becomes extremely important in Excel for order of operations with different equations. Excel can assist even the most dull of people to become functional at putting together something that resembles order and quantitative aptitude, even if it is a complete guise. For that reason, one must understand order of operations clearly and not drift from them:

1. *P*arentheses
2. *E*xponents
3. *M*ultiplication/*D*ivision
4. *A*ddition/*S*ubtraction

Do not forget order of mathematical operations in that specific order! If you are writing an equation in Excel, you need to remember where to put parentheses. For example, say your company did the following in revenue given the years below:

2012: $55,000,000 (OLD YEAR)
2013: $62,500,000 (NEW YEAR)

Your equation for year-over-year revenue growth in Excel is:

= (NEW – OLD) / OLD
= (62,500,000-55,000,000)/55,000,000

= 7,5000,000/55,000,000
= 0.1363

Slide the decimal over two places to convert to percentage... and *boom*!

= 13.63%, quite an interesting growth number.

If you forgot your parentheses, your equation would erroneously be performed as follows:

= NEW - OLD/OLD

Due to no parentheses in the line above, the order of operations would be *division and then subtraction*, resulting in the following:

= 62,500,000 – 55,000,000/55,000,000
= 62,500,000 – 1
= 62,499,999

The example above would easily be flagged by anyone besides maybe a government pervert watching porn all day on the taxpayer's dime. However, when typing long numbers, it could be easy to miss a zero somewhere, making the result possibly logical. Or one may be working with more complex equations and steps where the result will seem valid. The important thing is to be meticulous with the details of equations, know Excel, know PEMDAS, and check your work consistently. In my department, we have a little cheesy rallying cry, "How often do we audit? We constantly audit!" Despite the fromunda cheesiness of this line, it is an all-important tenet to any mathematical analysis. Careless errors are a killer.

With level 1 math, everyone working a corporate job can do it. It doesn't require you to be good at math or enjoy math. Performing level 1 math for those who don't enjoy it is sort of like taking one for the team, being the guy who hooks up with the not-so-cute girl so your buddy can have sex with the perfect ten. As a member of a corporation, they hired you to be a team player. Take one for the team, suck up your childhood insecurities from sack to throat, and become functional at level 1 math. Do not complain or openly declare how incompetent you are at math, because it only hurts your career and makes you appear insufficient for high-level positions.

Level 2

Don't *shart* your britches, sheeple. Level 2 math is nothing to be *scurred* of, but winners do get separated from losers. I have witnessed firsthand people be stuck on a level 2-word problem (or calculation) they cannot solve. They may have lacked confidence in their ability to perform the problem or lacked the intellect to conceptualize the problem. Regardless, level 2 math is something you need to be aware of in business along with your aptitude in this world. Below are a few examples of level 2 math as applied in the real world of business.

1. *Word problems*—We are out of kindergarten and into the frying pan. Ms. *Face Squat*, the sexy first-grade teacher, is no longer holding up a "6 + 9" flash card and revealing "69" stitched on the front of her panties like a scarlet letter. The answer is fifteen, jackass! Get your mind out of the gutter. Word problems cover a gambit of subject matter and ranges of difficulty. A big area for word problems in business is the what-if scenario. *What if we grew by X percent this year? How much would we need to average every day for the rest of the year to hit our goal? What would our margins be if we lower prices by $10 per unit? What about if we raise prices by $5 per unit? If demand drops by 5 percent after we raise prices by $10 per unit, will we be better off than if we had not raised prices at all? Can you put together a pricing model for gas and raw material prices along with breakeven points depending on a range of scenarios? What is the price elasticity of demand for our products?* If you're a stoner, I probably just lost you. But I'll proceed anyways and continue to mind fuck you some more. But what does it all mean? Is the company going triple rainbow? As you can see, there are a lot of what-the-fuck-if scenarios in business. The more insane the people you work with, the crazier and less logical

the scenarios can be, but to be a good analyst, one must fulfill dumb-shit requests at any given time. Remember, your persuasion (and income) is derived from quantitative analysis, not shutting down people's looney tune ideas.

2. *Algebraic expressions and solving equations*—Algebra is a fun subject. Forget how lame the elementary schoolteacher was teaching it. They probably weren't that good at math to begin with and definitely not at explaining it. Or maybe you were too busy perving on the girl who first developed womanly tits. Algebra is clear and concise. For the most part, in business math, you will need to solve for a variable. This is your unknown, usually represented with an X. Let's think of this in terms of business application. To begin, any addition, subtraction, multiplication, or division problem can be thought of as an algebraic expression, with the solution X being the unknown. For example, your porn distribution company has a daily sales average = \$56,400 for thirty days in the month of September. Your algebraic expression to find total revenue for the month becomes \$56,400 × 30 = X. Oh shit, you have to solve for X! Algebra—scary as picking up what you thought was a lady prostitute only to find a bulge in its, her—let's be honest—his panties!

   Problem Solving for September Sales:
   Solve for X.
   X= Monthly Sales
   Daily Sales Average × Number of Days = Monthly Sales
   \$56,400 × 30 = X
   X = \$1,692,000

Great Scott, Batman! You just solved for X! Give that fat, obnoxious math teacher you always hated a call and tell 'em you just dropped your balls (or tits) on X's face, Arabian-algebraic goggle style.

Let's rework the equation, so X moves around like that sneaky woman who used to cheat on you in the dorms. New question to solve: Your gross sales of bukkake porn were $1,500,000 for the month of September. Each video costs $5. How many total videos did you sell in the month of September, and what was your daily sales average in dollars and units?

Solve for X.
List all knowns:

1. Total Revenue = $1,500,000
2. Number of Days in September = 30
3. Video Cost per Unit = $5

List unknowns = X

1. Total Videos Sold = X
2. Daily Avg. Sales (number of videos)
3. Daily Avg. Sales (dollars)

Write algebraic equation:

1. Total Videos Sold = Total Sales Revenue / Cost per Video
    a. Total Videos Sold = $1,500,000 / $5 per video
    b. Total Videos Sold = 300,000 bukakke videos
    c. Holy cum cones Batman, that's a lot of filthy Asian porn!
2. Daily Avg. Sales for Number of Videos = Total Videos Sold / Number of Days in the Month
    a. Daily Avg. Videos Sold = 300,000 videos / 30 days in the month
    b. Daily Avg. Videos Sold = 10,000 bukakke videos per day!
    c. Who are these perverts buying this shit? Probably your local nonprofit leaders and politicians!

3. Daily Avg. Sales Dollars = Total Sales Revenue / Number of Days in the Month
    a. Daily Avg. Sales $s = $1,500,000 / 30
    b. Daily Avg. Sales $s = $50,000 per day

A tenet to live by is to not just audit, but *constantly audit*! Maybe your fat, sticky finger entered an extra zero in the calculator because you were so excited from the funnel cone porn. Let's audit by reversing the basic equations and check they add up to the original known factors in the word problem.

Audit 1—Answer was 300,000 total bukkake videos sold. We know they cost $5 per video. So 300,000 videos sold × $5 per video = $1,500,00 in total sales revenue. Our audit is correct! We were able to recalculate one of the original knowns from the initial problem.

Audit 2—We reverse the equation and check for logic. Our answer was daily average number of video sold was 10,000 per day. We know there are 30 days in the month, so 10,000 per day on average × 30 days in the month = 300,000 total perv videos sold.

Audit 3—Again, we work backward from our solution to the knowns from initial word problems. Our answer was the daily average sales in dollars was $50,000 per day times 30 days in the month = total sales revenue of $1,500,000. We arrive back to stated facts. Thus, our audit proves we did not make any mistakes.

Word problems and algebraic equations will become more complex and drawn out than the rudimentary examples above. You must have the ability to quickly calculate an average but also write, step by step, explain, and understand how a word problem translates into an algebraic expression. You must understand all pieces of an equation and how they interact. Always audit by rearranging the equation, plugging in your answer, and arriving back at the stated known facts (as we performed in the audits above). Sometimes the abridged version of quickly calculating an answer will suffice, but other times it will not. You must be near and farsighted when it comes to mathematics in the workplace. Sometimes you must be Israeli and take whatever office equipment you have to implement it to fight off those crazy long-beards shooting rockets into your corporate office. Other times you must be like the Russians stuck in frozen tundra and write an extensive encyclopedia about a business problem. Failure to have the ability to do both will leave you at a disadvantage. Then again, always remember to be American, with the intuition and pragmatism to do what is best in any given situation. Context, people, context.

3. *Understanding and dissection of key performance metrics (KPI's)*—"Our GM is 55 percent. Our DSA is $25,000. Our RPV is $15.55. Our YOY growth is 6.8 percent. Our BTAC are 34 DD." Yes, last acronym stands for "biggest tits at corporate." In business, you will find acronyms and esoteric jargon become the norm for certain companies and industries. Some people, knee-deep in the shitty side of corporate life, will throw out acronyms to sound smart. First off, don't force acronyms or be that guy or gal who uses acronyms superfluously. It makes you seem as a pretentious and robotic crony. You also have to sense it out company by company. Don't go straight into a new position and throw out there, "I need an answer by COB (close of books)" because in my thirty-plus years of life, I have only seen one person use that acronym in an email, and it seemed out of place. Communication is key, and most of the people who saw COB likely sat and thought, *What the hell is COB? Corn on the cob?* When starting a new job, be the second person to use an acronym, not first.

More important than blindly chanting numbers or key performance metrics is the ability to dissect and explain what they mean. For example, know the numerator and denominator of each KPI, so you can articulate at a deeper level than just, "RPV is $10.26." Understand that Revenue per Visit = $102,600 in total revenue divided by 10,000 visits. This metric indicates that you average $10.26 in revenue per visit to the company's website. This is a simple example, but as you begin to perform more financial statement and ROI analysis, the metrics can be tricky in what they measure.

4. *Conversions*—"We have ten thousand pounds of silicon in the warehouse," you proudly tell your boss after weighing inventory. He promptly replies, "Well, we need to know how many fake tits we can make. Pounds do us no good, you amateur! We need CCs! I want to know how many sets of 300CC tits we can make with that slippery silicon of WIP!" Swallow your nuts from your throat and gather yourself—it's time to convert! No, I don't mean converting to be a sexual deviant by cutting off your man parts! I mean converting between units of measure. Conversions can be multistep, so you need to get comfortable executing them from the simplest to the most complex. There has been a time in business when nobody in the entire office could perform a conversion calculation, and the problem was brought to my desk. Having the ability to perform multi-step conversions will set you apart from the crowd.

First things first. What is the problem you are trying to solve? List all the knowns and then X, your unknown. Sometimes the information may not be readily available on the conversion from pounds to CCs, and it may take multiple steps.

List the information available (i.e., *knowns*) needed to solve your problem:

1. 10,000 pounds of silicon in the warehouse
2. 16 oz. = 1 pound
3. 1 cc = 0.03381402 fl. oz.
4. 600 cc = a set (2 × 300cc) of nice fake tits!
5. How many sets (600cc total) of fake, silicone tits can we make with that WIP?

Solve:

1. Convert 10,000 pounds to ounces.
    a. 1 pound = 16 ounces

b. 10,000 pounds = 10,000 × 16 ounces
c. 10,000 pounds = 160,000 ounces

2. Convert ounces to CCs
   a. We know 1 CC= 0.03381402 ounces. How many CCs do you need for 1 ounce?
   b. Divide:
      i. 1 CC/0.03381402 ounces per CC = 29.57353 CCs needed to equal 1 ounce.
      ii. i.e., 1 ounce = 29.57353 CCs

3. From 1c. above: 160,0000 ounces = how many CCs?
   a. 160,000 ounces = 160,000 × (29.57353 CC's per liquid ounce)
   b. 160,000 ounces = 4,731,764.8 CCs.

4. Convert CCs to Sets of Silicone Tits (600CC=1 set):
   a. 600 CCs = 1 set of fake tits.
   b. 4,731,764.8 CCs = how many sets of fake tits?
   c. Divide:
      i. = 4,731,764.8 CCs / 600 CCs per set of fake tits
      ii. = 7,886.27 sets of 600 Cc fake tits!

5. Always check your work for rationality!
   a. List all your solutions and check against the known conversion:

Step	Your Solution	Based on Known Conversion(s)	Does this make sense?
1c.)	10,000 pounds = 160,000 ounces	1 pound = 16 ounces	*Yes!*
2b.)	1 ounce = 29.574353 CC	1 CC = 0.03381402 ounces	*Times both sides of known conversion by 29.574353 to check…say yes!*
3b.)	160,000 ounces = 4,731,764.8 CC	1 CC = 0.03381402 ounces, 1 ounce = 29.57353 CC	*Note, ounces are a fraction of cc in both cases, so yes! Or conversely, cc's are a multiple (X times) ounces, so yes! Double yes, shwing!*

4b.)	4,731,764.8 CC = 7,886 sets of 600 CC fake tits	600 CC = 1 set of fake tits	*Note 600:1 ratio for CC: set of fake tits. In the solution, this ratio is 4,731,764.8cc: 7,886.23 sets of tits: Divide both sides by 7,886.23 to check work. Yes!*

Some key tips and tricks for you when converting silicon pounds to sets of tits. First, when executing conversions, you only have two options—divide or multiply. For example, when converting from pounds to ounces and know 16 ounces = 1 pound. If you are solving for how many pounds are equal to 160,000 ounces, and uncertain which operation to perform, try to multiply ***and*** divide and then rationalize against your conversion to see which makes sense.

You know:
16 ounces = 1 pound
Solving for how many pounds is 160,000 ounces

Try to multiply:
160,000 ounces × 16 ounces per pound = 2,560,000 pounds?

Try to divide:
160,000 ounces / 16 ounces per pound = 10,000 pounds?

Check which of the two makes sense against the known conversion of 16 ounces being equal to 1 pound. When you multiplied, the result is 160,000 ounces being equal to 2.5 million pounds. That doesn't pan out because in the known conversion, the number of pounds is much less than the number of ounces. When you divided, the result is logical compared to the known conversion: 160,000 ounces equal to 10,000 pounds, ounces are greater than pounds. This coincides with the known conversion. Not trying to make this overly complex, but if you are a young professional petrified of math and with a silicon polluted mind, simplify and check your work. Always reference against the known conversion. Walk through each step and be boss hog about it. Put conversions into a methodical process with constants checks and references to help minimize errors. Get comfortable with the methodology of a corporate analyst, even if you work in client relations (or other less quantitatively oriented departments).

5. *Margin calculations and meanings for different business* segments—Margins rule business. A company crushing gross sales may not be as profitable as one with healthy margins. In business, profit margins (next to cash) are king and one of the most discussed metrics. As a consumer making a purchase, the easiest way to think of gross margin is in terms of how much above cost you pay for an item. For example, if you pay one hundred dollars for a leather set of crotchless chaps that cost a company ten dollars in material, you are paying ninety dollars in gross margin dollars to that company. Oftentimes, gross margin will be discussed in terms of a percentage since many companies will mark up an item based on its cost of goods sold. It is common to want to know what percentage of a sale can go toward profit after paying for the cost of materials and direct labor to produce it. To look at gross margin as a percentage: Gross Margin = (Revenue – COGS) / Revenue → ($100 - $10) / ($100) → 90 percent of the selling price is gross profit.

   The thing with gross margin is that it does not tell the whole story. It can lead executives into a false impression or comfort zone of how much money a company is making off a core product. "We sold $1,000,000 in silicon tits, 90 percent of that in profit!" Okay, take it easy, killer. You may have a 90 percent gross margin, but those nine hundred thousand in margin dollars do not make it to the bottom line, your net income. That is because other company expenses hit on top of the simple cost of goods sold. COGS only includes materials and direct labor costs associated with the production of a selling good. You have overhead expenses such as office rent, electricity, and administrative costs of running your operation that are not directly related to production of the item you sell. You have selling expenses. Your company has a sales team stuffing their tits (or wangs) in people's faces to demonstrate how neat the product is. You pay for advertising via online ads, print, and maybe billboards to keep it real old-fashioned. Hopefully, you invest a little in research and development for the latest technologies to keep your product relevant for the future. There are an array of other miscellaneous operating expenses: gas for transportation, tax-deductible meetings, travel costs, and whatever else not directly attached to the cost of goods sold.

Consider additional margin calculations. On a monthly, quarterly, and annual basis, net income margin will always be the most important. While it is an easy calculation (Net Margin = (Net Profit / Gross Revenue)), it isn't as popular as gross margin on the reg. It goes without saying that net income tracked on a monthly basis will tell a company if they are actually making more money and not just bringing in additional topline revenue. As a business leader, all actions and decisions should be with the intent of improving a company's net income margin. You can grow a company by one million dollars in sales, but if your operating expenses crept up to the tune of 1.2 million dollars to achieve that growth, you did not become more profitable. While net income is key, make sure you get a slice of the pie (via profit share, bonus structure tied to profitability or shares in the company), because if not then you really don't achieve more success when a company is growing.

It is simpleton work to only think of the day-to-day sales & profitability. Mismanagement of month-end and timely reporting for transactions can mean you are not correctly accounting for expenses that may come monthly, quarterly, or even once a year. Timely accounting for transactions and having a consistent frequency of month-end reviews can prevent profit-spoiling surprises—like thinking you can sneak a stomach bubble fart out at the office but end up needing a change of from-unda-wear!

One final slab of sausage for you to chew on regarding sales revenue and margins: Just because you made sales at a healthy margin does not mean that sale converts to cash. You will often have large customers with payment terms who will end up not paying for whatever reason. If that sales revenue doesn't convert to cash, then it was all for nothing. In fact, you will have to write it off as a loss in the end. Accounts receivable management means collecting from your customers and not sending out product when it poses a high risk for nonpayment. For this reason, having healthy credit checks on customers and a robust accounting department to collect accounts receivable is crucial for any corporation.

6. *Looking at raw data vs. blindly following* averages—One of the banes and miscalculations in economics and mathematics is being too reliant upon averages. Averages are formed at the center of bell curves. Breaking down bell curves into more specified segments can give you a drastically changed bell curve. Focusing too much on the average can make one blind to the extreme cases at the front or back end of that curve where truths may lie. Analyses can be uprooted by extremes from one side of the curve or another, with deeper segmentation unveiling different results. Scan raw data for anomalies from the get-go and be able to explain them. While the average provides insight into how the imaginary, average customer will behave, it can blind you to how your biggest dollar spenders behave. Think about it: There may not be a single customer who acted in the same way as your "average" result. This means you need to understand every dot within the bell curve to be truly enlightened. Those big-money clients are at the extreme front end of the bell curve, but if you lose them, it is a big loss to your income statement.

   Within each bell curve, there are different groups (or herds) of people that, if separated, could give a different-looking bell curve. Always consider a deeper level into which groups can be segmented. For example, if you are measuring revenue per visit to the website, look at different types of customers: new customers vs. returning, regional and country differences, male vs. female, different age groups, segmentation based on dollar spend, how they found your website, etc. If you are not looking at groups within groups and perusing the raw data that constructs an average, you miss key insights.

Think of it this way: If you planned on visiting a Latin country and someone told you the average woman is 4'11, with A cup tits and weighs one hundred eighty pounds, is that reason to assume you won't find a gem in that country? Absolutely not. There is a normal distribution, and maybe there is an age disparity in that country. If you break down that country's women into age groups, the eighteen- to twenty-five-year-old demographic is on average 5'2, one hundred ten pounds with C cup tits ever since milk was introduced to that population. Does that sound a little better for your visit? Of course! There could even be one thousand women in that country with DD-sized tits. Never throw the baby out with the bathwater of statistical averages, and always scan the raw data!

Since we live in the age of equal treatment, let me try and relate this to women (or males that identify themselves as females and are into wang). Pretend you are looking into a country's medical statistics, and it shows that on average, the wang size is two inches for a population. Would you, as a big wang lover, want to visit that area? Absolutely not. However, there is a normal distribution, and maybe there is an age disparity in that country. The old man group dominates, yet their limp wangs measure under an inch, greatly skewing the average. If you look at the eighteen- to twenty-five-year age group, you get normal wang sizes and some horse dongs within that group. You just never really know until dissecting every dot on a bell curve!

7. *Dynamic, applied analysis with proper* conceptualization—While this is not a regimented, number-crunching mathematical concept, it is a conceptual *concept* that needs *clarity. How's that for alliteration?* In mathematics, while hardcore number crunching is vital for success, equally or more so important is the ability to conceptualize the abstract and apply a dynamic, relevant mathematical line of reasoning of proper analysis. We have discussed timeframes for reporting in previous chapters, but what needs to be reiterated here is the ability to think about data sets, analyses, and mathematics from a dynamic point of view. What exactly does that mean? That means that you do not simply repeat the same process every year on the dot without exploring explanations for every square inch of analysis in an Excel spreadsheet. Paint a vivid story of the business into a masterpiece rather than a dull, mundanely square review that is blatantly obvious. Does that mean every analysis needs to be built from scratch? In some sense, yes. You may ask, "But why can't I just compare this December's sales to last year's sales for the same time period?" Well, jackass, because there may be circumstances affecting the comparison that are not explained just by running the numbers. There could be a spike in raw ingredient prices leading to a decline in profitability, a serious ailment or shift in wages of your primary client group that could impact demand, or a range of other possibilities to explain changes in metrics. In essence, think of every analysis as a holiday dish. Yes, you may have a dish that everyone has loved for the past ten years. However, if it is a dish traditionally baked in the oven, what do you do if the oven goes out? If it is a barbecued item, what happens if the grill takes a dive? Improve upon the existing dish. Can you add a paired item? Would a complimentary alcoholic beverage accent the flavor of this winning dish? What items do you serve with this dish? So it goes with business math analysis. Delve balls deep into the numbers and data. Bring them to life.

Level 3/4

Levels 3 and 4 are the math realms where good analysts live. It is where engineers live. It is where scientists and researchers live. It is the land of complex mathematics that ninety-nine percent of people will never put their tip into, let alone deeply penetrate. This isn't your local ma and pa cash register, "How much change do we give on a $23.56 bar tab if they hand us five five-dollar bills?" One dollar and forty-four cents, dipshit! That's a dollar bill, a quarter, a dime, a nickel, and four pennies. Always got to be thinking on the move, McFly!

High-level managers need to have a ten-thousand-foot view and understanding of the Level III and IV math realms as they apply to business. The reason I blend 3 and 4 is that once you reach a certain level of complexity in mathematics, some concepts must be ground into one's head. That means countless hours of study, repetition, practice, conceptualizing, learning the same thing in various methods, and putting in time and effort until, finally, the damn thing resonates. For the majority of people, they do not have the grit, intelligence (or combination of both) to achieve a true understanding at this level of mathematics. That is fine. It makes the scarce number of people that do valuable.

When running marketing cohort analysis, consumer behavior analysis, scientific research, A/B testing, and other various methods requiring statistical significance (and to be a boss hog), you need a general understanding of the following as they pertain to statistics:

What are statistics? What is the overall outlook and meaning of a statistical model when an employee comes to you with data and assumptions? How certain can you be that a statistical analysis is accurate and actionable? Will the numbers help guide and forecast for the future? Being in this ballgame for some time, I would look at statistics like this: while a general population forms bell curves, it does not always mean you should apply a peanut butter spread from that bell curve to your business application. If anyone has dated (in the era of the internets), it is clear that men are from Mars and women are from Venus. However, within each of those distinct planets, there are grave differences among the populations. And if you were going to try and just match up the men from Mars and women from Venus based on average interactions that lead to chemistry, very few from each planet's center bell curve would link up. This is how statistics are for business. It isn't a simple methodology. Be skeptical in a healthy, productive way. Understand that averages are just that, averages. There are anomalies that fall far away from the average. We have gone over this in previous chapters.

I think we have beaten this subject to death like a redheaded stepchild. The key here is that to be analytical, you don't have to be a mathematician. Yes, to be an analyst, you will need a foundation in statistics and an understanding of algebra and some deeper concepts than two plus two equals four. There are online tools to test statistical significance. The key is to have a general understanding of these concepts. It is like any sport you played (if you weren't a fat sow): it is all about the fundamentals. Think about Tim Duncan, multiple-time NBA Champion with the San Antonio Spurs. The guy was approaching one hundred years old and still playing at a very high level in the NBA. Why is that? His nickname gives you a hint: "The Big Fundamental." Never be stagnant and do not accept self-proclaimed stupidity from years of failure in elementary and high school math. Your brain may have developed since then and be able to grasp more concepts now. Take a look; it's all in a book, *Reading Rainbow.* You betcha!

The good news is you can take the following advanced mathematical concepts and sit on 'em, then rotate: advanced engineering math, advanced calculus, differential equations, advanced physics, mechanics, etc. To be successful in business, you won't need any of that in your playbook, unless you are an engineer in a field that requires it. Good luck, padawans! Pull out your Jedi sticks and go get some.

Chapter 7

TECHNOLOGY, MY BALLS

TECHNOLOGY. WHAT A BUZZWORD AND, SOMETIMES, A buzz-kill. Ever met an IT guy who acted like the world's smartest human, only to find out ninety percent of his job entails restarting a server? Maybe you have yet to peek behind the Wizard of Oz but trail them for a day of "troubleshooting." Sometimes, that's it—a job as easy as restarting a computer. In fact, I did work in IT for some time, installing new software and hardware systems, running reports against physical inventory cycle counts, and yes, restarting servers to fix eighty percent of people's tech problems. Let's put it this way: my IT-Operations role at a large distribution center came to an end when I had an altercation with one of the warehouse workers we had been using for temp labor. Initially running operations, I transitioned into IT when the executives moved in and systems needed to be installed.

While implementing inventory management and tracking systems, I needed employees to provide daily physical counts to audit against. This forty-year-old-plus, semi-wannabe Latino tough guy was not giving me cycle counts at all. I had asked him repeatedly, and he kept neglecting his job duties. I was young and full of—well, testosterone, shall we say. I called him into my office and said straightforwardly, "Look, I have asked you numerous times for daily, physical inventory counts so I can audit against the system. I've given you the template to fill out, etc. I don't want to hear any more excuses. I want the inventory counts. That's it. End of story." My tone was how any twenty-four-year-old's would be when a subordinate blatantly disobeys and disrespects you. This was much earlier in my career, and I didn't have time for bullshit.

The grown man left the room, and I thought, "Okay, I'll be getting my physical counts soon. Good deal." A couple of minutes later, this motherfucker storms into my office and stands there, fuming. "Hey, bro, I don't like that tone you used with me, aye! Don't fucking talk to me like that!" I casually asked him what he wanted to do about it, and he wanted to step outside. With my blood boiling, I went out to the front of our corporate office doors, facing him mono e mono. Mind you, I have a few loose screws, and when it comes to fighting, I immediately snap. He talked some shit, so I bench-pressed him in the chest, slamming him back into the corporate office doors, just recently opened for business. I proceeded to give him my address and told him where to meet me at five if he wanted to fight like a man. He had likely served time in jail, but at the end of the day, he was a real pussy. I've never backed down from a scrap, have never lost in one, and have never beat up someone who didn't deserve it. Fighting is part of my DNA.

So where was I going with this story? Oh, that's right: technology. Most of it was mindless work. After this altercation, I was done. I opted to buy a Harley, cruise it to work my last two weeks, break my apartment lease, and live off a nice severance for a few months. Not to say all IT is mindless work. Computer programming is pure logic, complex, and requires rational thinking to become functional at it. That is why most irrational people do not understand it. Troubleshooting from a call center, installing updates, installing a router and modem, fixing a printer, or helping someone with their basic computer needs are all pain-in-the-ass jobs. It often requires more customer service and patience than any deep thinking. But IT is a very broad area that requires understanding the different business areas.

Let's clarify the different areas of informational technology you can be involved in. First, many IT and database managers mostly restart servers. If you want to get a two-year tech degree and do this, it is a lax gig. You can get in with a good company, learn their systems and how to install them easily, and become the point man for whenever people in the office have trouble or need software programs installed. I've been downloading and installing software since elementary school (when computers and the internet first hit the market). If you are adept at navigating a computer with basic logic, this isn't the worst path. I wouldn't say it is the most mentally challenging or fun job. You are constantly doing customer service and fixing people's problems while dealing with their stress. An outgoing, personable personality will help you on this path. Think of being a branded car with "I'll fix your computer" stickers all over it. Some person brings you a laptop infected with viruses. You download, install, and run a thorough virus scan. Or you research the type of virus it is in their registry and how to remove it. Or you just format the hard drive and install the operating system from scratch. The good thing about this role is that you don't necessarily even need a degree and can earn a decent living. It just is up-and-down work, unless you catch on with a good company and that role grows.

A higher level of profession is to be a programmer in one of the many computer languages. My personal experience with programming (*that has proved most beneficial for a career in analytics*) has been writing SQL. SQL stands for Structured Query Language and is basically a database with field names and rows of data that look like an Excel spreadsheet. It exists on the back end of transactional programs with set computer command statements to query, alter, and manipulate the database by entering proper computer language and executing the statement. To delve into computer programming, you need to overcome the hump of thinking of computer software and programs as only what exists on the front end. For example, when you log in to Instagram, what you see is the front-end user interface (even though all these ONLYFANS girls now promote their back ends-trash). On the back end is where the computer programming exists that created that front-end view you are accustomed to interacting with. The back end is a whole new world of beauty.

In SQL, fields are column header names populated with data you can read across at the row level. SQL is great for managing relational databases. Relational databases are a way of organizing data into multiple tables with common fields that you can join. Without separating out those databases, every transaction would have to populate every single field for every transaction, even when a field was not relevant. It would create a computing nightmare, and computers would crash more than they already do.

For example, in one of your SQL tables, it may have all customer information; in another, all order totals information; and in another, line items on every order. These databases are at different levels, but there is a relationship that ties each database to one another, usually. This is not always the case. However, below demonstrates the case of relational databases in a mock SQL table I drew up in Excel.

CUSTOMER.DBO

Customer ID	Customer Name	Phone Number	Profile Description	Customer's Lifetime Spend
1	Stinky Fingers	805-666-6969	Homeless dude that smells like shit	$ 305.00
2	No Balls	805-143-1431	Dbag that calls from payphone	$ 350.00
3	Dingle Berry	805-696-4444	Typical sheeple	$ 495.00
4	Dirk's Diggler	999-999-6969	Loves to show off the girls he spanks	$ 180.00
5	Big Tits Betty	805-444-6969	Gets high and rides savage men	$ 625.00

ORDERS.DBO

Customer ID	Order Number	Order Total	Order Date	Order Status	Payment Type
1	1266	$ 160.00	1/12/2016	Paid	Cash
2	1267	$ 330.00	1/22/2016	Paid	Cash
3	1268	$ 470.00	2/1/2016	Paid	Cash
4	1269	$ 45.00	2/11/2016	Paid	Cash
4	1270	$ 90.00	2/21/2016	Paid	Check
5	1271	$ 45.00	3/2/2016	Paid	Check
5	1272	$ 130.00	3/12/2016	Paid	Cash
5	1273	$ 450.00	3/22/2016	Pending	Credit Card
1	1274	$ 100.00	4/1/2016	Pending	Credit Card
1	1275	$ 45.00	4/11/2016	Paid	Cash
2	1276	$ 20.00	4/21/2016	Paid	Cash
3	1277	$ 25.00	5/1/2016	Paid	Cash
4	1278	$ 45.00	5/11/2016	Paid	Cash

ITEMS.DBO

Order Number	Line Item #	SKU	Description	SKU Price	Quantity
1266	1	MJANE8	MARY JANE 1/8TH	$ 45.00	1
1266	2	BKUSH8	BLUEBERRY KUSH 1/8TH	$ 45.00	1
1266	3	RSNOIL1	RESIN OIL 1 GRAM	$ 35.00	2
1267	4	GRND10	GRINDER 10 GRAMS	$ 15.00	2
1267	5	BNANA8	BANANA DREAM 1/8TH	$ 60.00	1
1267	6	STRBK1OZ	STRAWBERRY KILLER 1 OZ.	$ 240.00	1
1268	7	MNGOK4	MANGO OG 1/4 OZ	$ 90.00	1
1268	8	GRLSKT1OZ	GIRL SCOUT COOKIES 1 OZ.	$ 350.00	1
1268	9	HMPBR24OZ	HEMP BEER 24 OZ.	$ 3.00	10

What does it all mean? Are you seeing a double rainbow? Holy shit, it's going triple! Time to take a trip to the dark side—the back end of software programs: relational databases. As you can see in the three mock SQL tables above, one has customer information, another order information, and another items-on-orders information. You can also see that there is information that ties one database to another. For example, in customer.dbo and orders.dbo, both have a field labeled "Customer ID." In the customer.dbo table, "Customer ID" only appears once for each customer and contains unique information that has been input on the front end of a computer program about that individual. In the table orders.dbo, "Customer ID" shows up multiple times, once for every order that individual has placed. In database architecture, you would be able to join the customer.dbo and orders.dbo tables by linking up the field "Customer ID" that exists in both tables.

In SQL, you can write commands that yield results based on the logic you define within those commands. There are set commands that perform different functions on datasets: select, join, insert, delete, etc. With proper syntax, you can run queries that select all orders greater than a certain dollar amount or only orders from a certain customer. Think of it as a language that allows you to "filter" while also applying more powerful commands to databases, such as joining (with another database), inserting new columns, writing customized calculated fields, and a myriad of other actions. SQL is a command language—you can write commands to datasets. It is very powerful. We will not discuss proper syntax for SQL here, but know that once you start having a fundamental grasp of the SQL language, your toolbox for analysis (*and ability to report on any business transactions*) will fundamentally change forever. Welcome to the dark side of transactional software.

Change your underwear, wipe your ass with wet wipes. It's time for a fundamentally new view of computer programs. What you see isn't always what you get. Maybe your IT department and company only allow access to the front-end reporting in their software programs. If that's the case, you are missing out. This is a very narrow, obsolete view of reporting on transactional history. Business needs change daily; different stories need to be analyzed and told. One cannot rely on the generic, canned "reports" button or dropdown. Big whoop—you can run a few basic reports based on what the creator of that program thought would be important. Imagine having access to the entire dataset on the back end, being able to join tables and write queries for anything you can imagine to dissect that dataset. You aren't limited to date ranges, narrowed views, or rigid reporting that doesn't suit your needs. If there is data being captured, you have access to it on the back end. This is about the only time I enjoy back-end access. In my opinion, the back end of human anatomy is an exit hole, not an insertion point. To each their own, but the exit hole should be kept impeccably clean with water and soap. Read some Jack Kerouac; he agrees.

Maybe you're asking yourself, "Why doesn't all this data live in a single table? And why can't I just use filters for all the data like I'm used to filtering on dating sites? Why can't I have unlimited back-end access to SQL tables?" The answer to all these questions is performance. On a fundamental level, a computer runs slow when you either (1) get a virus from watching too much granny porn or (2) fill your computer's memory with too much data. When your computer has too much data, running a command, executing a program, or searching for something requires searching through a much larger stack of bullshit (your full memory) to find or execute what you are trying to do. The same applies to computer software programs. If you have massive tables on the back end of a program, it will take long periods of time to execute commands and transactions. That is where the necessity for relational databases comes into play. Let's go back to our example above. Imagine if all three of these databases were combined into one. Every time a line item on an order was populated, that row would also populate all order info and detailed customer info. The dataset would grow exponentially, causing a bogged-down experience for anyone trying to operate on the front end of the software. The result of every single transaction in any of those databases would populate all the rows below across every row, even when certain rows were not necessary to record. The result is a giant database.

See below for a single, flat database that would record all fields any time any transaction happened, anywhere. Every single transaction would populate fifteen fields instead of the five or six fields applied to relevant tables above. Crash city! Hence, we need relational databases!

Disclaimer: Multiple join SQL table did not make final edits due to size. Google search large SQL query with multiple joins and many columns of results to get an idea of potential scope and issues it would cause systems.

Now it should be clear how one row of data looks if the back end of a software program did not live in a relational database. A single SQL table for our example would yield multiple, unnecessarily repeated fields for any transaction. Every time a line item was populated on an order, the back end would capture all of the fields from the orders.dbo and customer.dbo, even though they are just repeating data already known and stored separately. This SQL table would clog the database on the back end like a gerbil in Richard Gere's mouse trap, and the performance would be slow as molasses.

It isn't that you cannot get that single view from the relational database structure in SQL. You get the same outcome by joining the separate databases via query command language—customer.dbo to orders.dbo on the field "Customer ID" and orders.dbo to items.dbo on the field "Order Number." But you do this in an external Microsoft SQL Server program that doesn't impact your software once the query is executed and results are displayed. *Important note*: The execution of queries from Microsoft SQL Server can crash databases and your software if you try to pull too much data. I'm sure every developer has learned this early on at some point in their career. I know I did. The important point now is understanding the reason for relational databases in SQL: duplication of stored data on the back end creates performance issues. Relational databases are the Viagra that keeps software pumping at peak performance.

Now you understand the reason for relational databases and why they are separated on the back end. Let's discuss the power of

SQL commands to rearrange, put back together, join, add calculated fields, rename, insert, delete, and form these databases back into a perfectly submissive, 100 percent controlled entity as the end result. As a dominant person always looking for a good sub, the logic provided by SQL programming provides me with that. If you don't know what I'm talking about (because your sex life consists of poking it through the boxer hole missionary style), bear with me a bit more. SQL isn't for everyone. Some people like being the submissive one, held hostage to relying on others to form logic and provide them with the answers to their business questions. Cut that shit and embrace the power of SQL!

A primary capability of SQL commands is the ability to take segmented, relational databases and join them back together if they share a common field. Since the front-end view isn't always conducive to getting the analysis you need in its existential form, you may need to join databases to understand a full picture, i.e., join the customers database with the items database so you can see the different types of joints that a homeboy is smoking. If you only had data from the customers database, you wouldn't know the specific items they were purchasing; and if you just had the items database, you wouldn't have the customer information. That's why you need to know the fields from each database to join so you can get the full picture.

This is where something comes into play that can be applied to your career in general: longevity. Yes, that's right. Longevity with a specific company makes you more powerful in SQL because your understanding of schema—where different points of data exist and how they relate to one another—grows with time. Give your balls a tug and find out where different data lives, what you have access to, how databases are structured on the back end, which fields to join when writing queries, and the sort of reporting that is relevant to your business.

Some say it takes three years before an employee begins adding value in the form of real ROI to a company. I think that is probably accurate for average employees. If you are a badass in business with a lot of experience, you should be able to start adding value immediately after your cost of training. You can start adding value from day one in the form of positive vibes and culture enhancement in the office. Show up to work with a smile, be nice to people, give compliments, and start digging in to learn where the data exists that you need access to. Become friends with the people who have carte blanche access to the databases. If nobody does, start making suggestions about the reporting you would like to see. Inquire whether that information is being captured and by what software platform. Then investigate the front-end reporting that everyone has access to and assess its limitations. Be creative and think of everything being captured, where it lives, in what format, and come up with an action plan to put those pieces together in a way that is valuable.

That is the value of technology. It isn't about having a fancy iPhone that makes you look like a metrosexual. Technology adds value when it makes someone's life easier. Sure, having this elaborately designed integrated social media piece on your website that sells shoes may seem like a cool idea in smoke-filled rooms, but at the end of the day, customers may just want to come to your website to order a pair of Nike Air Force Ones. They don't want to jump through the hoops of setting up a profile, password, login, or any of that bullshit. They don't want to deal with the hassle of giving out personal information that could be sold to marketing companies. Give customers options for what level of engagement they want to have with your company. Never assume, because it makes an ass of u and me.

If you want to analyze databases and their structure, you must think spatially. Remember playing with building blocks, puzzles, Legos, Lincoln Logs, Transformers, or Tetris as a kid? That is how you can piece together the datasets on the back end of software programs. As Spider-Man would advise, upon the advice of his uncle, "With great power comes great responsibility." Don't think you get carte blanche access to SQL data tables and can go playing in them like an elementary school sandbox. You could severely damage your company if you are not careful and don't have fundamental programming knowledge in place.

The first fundamental is understanding that by querying the back end of a software program, you can make the front end of that program crash. Yes, your tinkering in the back-end tables of a website database can crash the website, preventing potential customer visits, causing lost sales, and requiring expensive software engineers to fix it. You have the power to completely freeze what is happening on the front end of any software program when operating in SQL. Think of it this way: have you made a female orgasm from touching her somewhere besides her vagina? Think of the vagina as the front end of a complex software system. Everyone operates in the vag. It is what everyone thinks of and imagines when talking orgasms. However, you can make that V cum by stimulating other areas, such as inner thighs, clitoris maximus, butt wiggling, or somewhere else that only you and she know about. The same goes for software and SQL table back-end querying. If you write a query that pulls together too much information on the back end, you can cause that program to crash—orgasm—on the front end. Most people don't know where you touched to cause that orgasm—crash—to the software system, but it happened. Just know it will cause severe problems (*and make you look like a jackass*) when the troubleshooting fix reveals you are the one to blame.

Treat the back-end SQL tables of a computer software program as you would a homey's girlfriend. You aren't there to make her orgasm and fall apart. You don't want to break up existing relational databases. You are there to be a good patron and extremely careful. Stick within your capabilities and always have a test (*non-live*) environment you can work in before messing with live databases.

Technology, my balls. Don't get caught up in the hype. I grew up in the era of dial-up internet, Yahoo unregulated chat rooms, and floppy disk command-driven Apple II GS computers. The fundamentals are all still in place. Yes, there are different computer programming languages better suited for different needs, but don't let IT be some big anal hole you avoid familiarizing yourself with because it is too complex. It is simpler than most people lead it on to be. Many times your IT DB Manager will restart a server and grossly exaggerate it as some complex process, claiming some technical error occurred and they had to debug. He or she literally just restarted a server.

Is there technology we can't even fathom on the way? Absolutely. Should it scare you? Well, if your skills aren't valuable, then maybe. If you are original, have passion, and keep yourself up to date on technology as it relates to your profession, you will be just fine. Will artists be rendered extinct during the technology age? We are in a tech-driven business environment, and graphic design artists are in high demand. Artists continue to be extremely relevant in the tech business. Until we face a Terminator-like scenario where our world is comprised of machines trying to kill men and women, keep your occupation and profession valuable and in line with technological trends. And if you don't, then don't complain when your 1800s-style pastel portraits are selling for pennies on the dime in downtown San Francisco. Petition local government for more welfare and grants for those who want to make a career out of something the market doesn't demand. But that is straight pussy shit.

There are other key technology tenets you must follow. First, do not become chained to any one specific technology. The older the company, the higher this risk becomes. Technology platforms and suppliers come and go. Companies will tend to customize software to cater to their specific business needs. They will usually have an in-house IT department that continues doing this as requests come up from different departments and as executives see fit. Having a customized software platform can improve your business model. It can help you analyze your business performance quickly, target and react to customers more efficiently, and expedite business processes based on your model. But the more customization, the more at risk you become of being tied to a "legacy system." A legacy system is one you stay on because it has been so heavily invested in, customized, and accustomed to that no one can just let it go.

For example, you may have an e-commerce platform. B2B customers make a request for specific reporting capabilities: "It sure would be nice if I could see marijuana sales by month and have those exported into QuickBooks. That way we could quickly report to the IRS for tax filings." Okay, so existing software doesn't have that capability as an "out-of-the-box feature." A company with a viable IT department would be able to do some customized development, integrate the existing software's API (application programming interface) with QuickBooks' API, and satisfy the customer's request to export to QuickBooks. An API is the schema that lives on the back end of software and allows two software programs to communicate and integrate with one another. If your software has a robust, well-coded API, you will be able to integrate with other software applications more easily. APIs are key in business because of the need for existing software to connect with other business software applications. A very basic example of this is if you are shipping your legalized weed through an order management software system, but decide you want to become integrated with FedEx or UPS's API so that you can calculate real-time shipping rates and track your shipments to update customers.

Understand business needs and how the puzzle pieces fit together. When customizing software and integrating with other software applications, it is key to understand that every custom development further chains a company from any future moves or upgrades that don't include the legacy software. With each new customized development comes, "Man, we can't move away from this software because we have this one cool feature we developed in-house that allows us to tickle customers' balls when they place an order." A company has the tendency to become tied to its existing software platforms, especially when customized developments were created in-house. The omnipresent threat is new, better software hitting the marketplace, and your company is too tied up in shackles—to the bedpost—of its existing software. This scenario of attachment, both psychological and systematic, to customizations means resistance to upgrade, even when necessary to stay relevant. Yes, software and platform changes are a big challenge. The integration process can be a pain in the ass. You may not have all the exact features your company is used to (and people may complain), and you will have to teach some salty dogs new tricks. All the experts of your current software platform become newbies once a company takes the leap into upgrading its technology.

Another key part of technology is that it isn't all programming. Don't ever tell someone, "I'm not a tech person." It automatically discounts you when you may be able to play a valuable role in the development of your company's software platform and technology. You may be playing five-on-two with yourself now, gasping, "How am I a tech person? I studied Cultural Anthropology-Gender Studies and work in sales as a tranny fanny promoter. I hate tech!" Sales and marketing are vital to technology. They are expected to be as in tune with the customer as anybody, while IT programmers are locked up in a cage in the back office eating Cheetos and writing code. The IT team may not be all that in touch with the real world and loyal customers that bring revenue to keep the lights on in your company's building.

For this reason, it is key that technology is guided by a visionary. The person writing the code may not have a strong grasp of the business needs. He or she may not be in touch with the customer. They may not even be in touch with pop culture and the types of things different generations gravitate toward. Ideally, a technology person would be great at understanding the business, understanding the marketing, understanding user experience, being able to write code, and having a grand vision for how to marry the technology with your company's core functionalities. But in business, there are departments and specialists. Mr. Tech Guy or Gal may not be reading customer comments and doing segmentation analysis all day. Good technology demands the involvement and considerations of all departments and specialties.

Technology is also meant to make people's lives simpler, not more complex. This is a key tenet to keep at the front of your mind when developing technology tools for your business. Yes, there are all kinds of cool apps, games, e-commerce platforms, websites, interactive experiences, virtual reality, etc. Do not let your imagination get out of the scope of what is necessary for the business. Think about the most basic example of how technology has improved efficiencies in the marketplace: utility bills. What was the old-school way of paying for your utilities? The electric company would monitor your usage, write up a bill, send it in the mail, you would open your bill, detach the payment coupon, write a check, send the coupon and check back via snail mail, and upon receipt, they would deposit your check. Think about all the time and effort that went into processing payments for utility bills back in the day. Some people may still go by this old-school methodology, but technology has created the potential for this entire transaction to be hands-free. With technology, you can do a single-time setup, save your payment information, and schedule automatic payments that pull money from your account when due. So basically, that entire process of paying utility bills has been simplified and almost reduced to nothing after initial setup. However, it doesn't mean that people want a social media network and profile when they simply want to pay their bill.

This is the right mentality to have when applying technology to your business. Explore what your customer is doing now. Think of ways that you could simplify or help them get what they need. Yeah, there are certain instances when people become engaged or hooked into certain social and community networks. However, always stick to what your core business is and improve upon that first. Don't try to expand your company's technology scope to be everything to everyone. There is already *a Farcebook, Tweeter, Instadouche,* and *Tinderella.* There may be some cool aspects of those apps that you can take into consideration, but it doesn't mean you want to force play having a website that sells hammers mandate a username and profile so that someone going to buy hammers has to upload a picture and become a part of your hammer social media community.

Think about technology in the right way. Understand it. Grasp it. Discover current trends and capabilities. But at the end of the day, be true to your business and what has made it great. Stay true to the fact that a customer is a real person who has come to your company for something. Make it as easy as possible for them to get what that thing is.

Chapter 8

TIME VALUE OF MONEY

WHAT IS WORTH MORE: $1 TODAY OR $1 a year from now? A dollar is a dollar, right? No, dumbass. That $1 today could be put in a bank and earn interest for an entire year. Yes, our crony federal reserve sets non-free-market interest rates, but 1 percent is better than zero. And $1 today could be $1.10 a year from now if you earned 10 percent interest. Which is more valuable—$1 today or that same $1 a year from now? Now you are getting with the program.

Forward thinking: how does this impact a business if you are a buyer vs. a seller? The perspective will determine the proper thought process in terms of settling payments. From the buyer's perspective: *Golly gee willikers, if I don't have to pay this hooker $60 for the hand job I get today, then I can put my $60 in the bank and earn interest. Whatever interest I earn from now until payment time, I will get to keep. Then the hooker gets her $60, and I keep my interest earnings!* Fantastic. Never pay a hooker if you don't have to!

And from the seller's perspective, say you are a hooker: Do you want your wrinkle-balled customer to pay today for an old-fashioned HJ, or do you want them to pay six months from now? Even a hooker knows to get paid before providing sexual services to guarantee payment! There are hookers who bail on services, hustling old dudes for cash. But that is beside the point. A hooker doesn't think about time-value-of-money principles but should. Anyone engaging in marketplace transactions should. From a time-value-of-money perspective, whoever has $60 today can put that shit in a bank and earn interest. If the hooker doesn't receive payment today—but six months from now—she (or he) is missing out on interest they could have earned during that time period.

Okay, a hooker can earn a few pennies of interest over the course of a year for getting paid upfront for giving an HJ to a semihard wang with a saggy scrotum. That service provider will likely buy cocaine and never think about the bank and interest rates. So don't be a hooker. Always be thinking of these general concepts: when you have to pay and how much you pay in interest. It will help you grasp the big picture in business finance, both personally and professionally.

In what cases would you want to pay cash up front, therefore avoiding interest? In what cases would you want to take out debt financing, paying back what you borrowed plus a set interest amount? Really, it depends on the personal financial situation. I'm going to provide general guidelines and considerations. First, any time you can take out a 0 percent interest loan and pay it back over time, that is a great time to do so. Why would someone want to go into debt, one may ask? I'll give the example of my Amazon store card that charges 0 percent interest if you pay back what you purchase within the set timeframe (usually around six months).

All right, you've splurged on Amazon as you usually do (*since your girlfriend doesn't make you splurge from motionless, missionary sex*). Let's say you spent $500 on one of those Japanese sex robots that look and feel like a real woman (*or man*). You have $500 in the bank and could easily just fork out the dough and be done with the transaction. That's it. Charge a debit card, close the deal, and never make another payment on that toy ever again. The second option is to exploit Amazon's 0 percent financing on purchases and pay back over a set amount of time.

As Amazon, you prefer to get the cash right now from the customer. Why? Well, it all goes back to the principles of banking and interest rates. If you pay Amazon cash now, they put that money in the bank (*or money market*) and start earning interest right away. See table below:

Year 0	$ 500.00
Annual Interest Rate	5 percent
Interest Earned	= 5 percent of $500 = $25
Year 1	$ 525.00

Not like we have 5 percent interest rates on savings now, but back in the day, that was considered normal. Hell, in the 1980s, you could easily have seen 15 percent to 20 percent savings rates. That made growing money via interest a lot easier if you had cash to save. It is clear above that if you paid Amazon $500 for a sex robot, that transaction could be $525 in Amazon's bank after a year of earning interest.

Please see below, in tabular form, Amazon's interest earning potential on the cash when you make $41.67 payments over the course of 12 months, totaling $500.

a) Month number	b) Monthly payment	c) Months of 5 percent annual interest?	d) Percentage of full year of $41.67 at 5 percent interest	e) 5 percent annual interest
1	41.67	12	= 12/12 = 100 percent	$2.08
2	41.67	11	= 11/12 = 92 percent	$1.91
3	41.67	10	= 10/12 = 83 percent	$1.74
4	41.67	9	= 9/12 = 75 percent	$1.56
5	41.67	8	= 8/12 = 67 percent	$1.39
6	41.67	7	= 7/12 =58 percent	$1.22
7	41.67	6	= 6/12 = 50 percent	$1.04
8	41.67	5	= 5/12 = 42 percent	$0.87
9	41.67	4	= 4/12 = 33 percent	$0.69
10	41.67	3	= 3/12 =25 percent	$0.52
11	41.67	2	= 2/12 = 17 percent	$0.35
12	41.67	1	= 1/12 = 8 percent	$0.17
	$500			$13.54

Take another gander at the table above. Focus. Pretend it's a big set of tits, or a stuffed sock in the pants (for you ladies). If you look at column b, that represents your monthly payment over the course of a year, totaling $500. Don't mind rounding issues for now. We're sticking to whole numbers above. In column c, you have the number of months interest you can earn 5 percent on that $41.67. The above table assumes Amazon gets paid on the last day of the previous month. In column d), as you work down, you see the percent of that full year's worth of 5 percent interest on $41.67 that you'd be able to earn. For example, if you look at month twelve, you only earn one month's worth of 5 percent interest for a full year. So 1/12 = 8 percent of what you would have earned for a full year of interest on the $41.67.

To state it clearly, instead of getting your $500, putting it in a bank, and earning 5 percent interest for a year totaling $25, if you accept a payment plan, you aren't able to earn that full amount of interest. And if you run the arithmetic from the table above, you only earn $13.54 of interest if you accept twelve monthly payments and invest each payment into savings for the same time period. This is versus the $25 of a full year's interest you could have collected upfront. On top of that, you have to take a risk of accounts receivable that may turn into bad debt if the customer doesn't pay. While the difference between $25 and $13.54 in interest may seem small, if we're talking $5 million in customer payments, the interest earning potential is $250K vs. $135.4K, so you could be leaving $114.6K on the table.

Simplified

- If I sell a $500 sex robot and receive payment *now*, put it in a bank, and earn 5 percent interest:
    - After a year, I will have $525 total ($500 initial investment + 0.05 × $500)

- If I sell a $500 sex robot, receive twelve payments of $41.67, each time putting the $41.67 in a bank:
    - After a year, I will have $513.54 (each $41.67 payment will yield a different percentage of a full year's interest of 5 percent).

Any lightbulbs coming on? Any tingling sensations in your balls? Here are the takeaways.

1. On the consumer side, never pay for anything now that you can later for the same price! You can always take that money you have now, put it in a bank, and earn interest. When you go to pay for that item later, you will have more cash available thanks to the interest you earned.
2. From a seller's side, your best-case scenario is to always accept cash payment upon delivery of service or goods. If you can receive early payment, even better. Invest that cash on hand. Earn a return.

Without going too much into financial statements, there is something that needs to be said for accounts receivable. An account receivable is when someone owes you money for a good or service you have already provided. A percent of accounts receivable will turn into bad debt, requiring a write-off on those accounts at a loss. Say you're accepting $41.67 payments on a French Polynesian sex robot you sold and allowed the customer to finance at 0 percent. There is always the risk that the customer will go bankrupt, go rogue, go to the grave, or go to jail for some perverse act. In any of those cases, you may never receive payment. The flow of financial statements would be: you earned revenue on the income statement when you sold the robot for $500 and delivered it, the $500 would sit on your balance sheet as an accounts receivable asset (with the liability your customer will default on payment) and convert to cash (the best asset) as payment is received in $41.67 increments. Balance sheet transaction would be Credit AR asset (decrease) and Debit cash asset (increase) as payments are received. If that account defaulted on payment, you would convert that account receivable liability into an expensed loss, and it would negatively impact your income statement.

When you allow customers to finance at 0 percent, you both: (1) miss out on the interest you could have earned on the total amount you would have accepted upfront and (2) take the risk of having an account receivable sit on your balance sheet, which could turn into a bad account (if the customer defaults on payment), requiring an expense to the income statement. On the flip side, as a customer, you always want to accept zero-percent financing because: (1) the money that would have gone toward the purchase can sit in a bank and earn interest, and (2) your cash flow doesn't take a hit all at once. For some people, a $500 hit to their cash flow doesn't mean much, but on large transactions, the same principles apply. From a savvy financial perspective, you live and die by interest rates, analyzing cash flow, timing of transactions, and putting your money to work so it brings you a return.

By now the time value of money should make sense. Today, $1 could be turned into $1.05 a year from now if you put it in a bank and earn 5 percent annual interest. So what's worth more? Today's $1 or that same $1 one year from now? If I'm a seller, I always want that dollar today. If I'm a buyer, I always want to pay that dollar later. And the reason all goes back to who gets to earn interest on that dollar. A dollar today is more valuable than a dollar in the future because of the earning potential—via interest—that you begin earning on $1 today. In business school, one of the first questions our finance professor asked was, "What is worth more, $1 today or $1 a year from now?" Of course, he was premising the question on the basis of looking at the earning power of interest rates. If you wanted to be a douchebag know-it-all, you could throw in the rise and fall of the dollar in global currency exchange markets and how that would impact your purchasing power for international goods. One may include inflation analysis and how the dollar's purchasing power can be impacted over the course of a year. But we are being by-the-book finance guys. The basic maxim for the time value of money is the earning power of interest rates.

Let's open a new world of you being a savvy financial being. All you need is Excel, the Internet, and a sliver of motivation to not be a deadbeat. Hell, fundamental financial concepts are not uber-complex. With all the online calculators and computer programs available, one can do a hell of a job faking their way through, even if one blows balls at math and number crunching. What do you need to consider when making a financial decision?

- *Interest rates*—The lower the interest rate you pay, the better; but conversely, the higher the interest rate, the more you can earn if you put that money into a bank. This means the interest rate environment will impact your purchase twofold. First, if interest rates are high, it should discourage you from making a purchase and paying back more than the sticker price over time. Second, the higher the interest rates, the more it should encourage you to hold onto that money and put it in a bank to earn interest on savings.

- *The future environment of interest rates*—For the past several years, the Federal Reserve has held interest rates artificially low. What does that mean? Well, it means savings in a bank won't earn you a significant return. It also means you have cheap access to cash. One won't have to pay much interest over time for smaller purchases, depending on the interest rate. On large purchases, such as a home, one will pay a substantial amount in interest over time, even with low rates. But the same principles apply: low-interest rates, borrow! Lower interest rates hit, refinance! And while we won't go balls deep into bonds, it needs to be stated. Since bonds (treasury bills) are a very common investment, you need to know that if interest rates rise, your bond price goes down. That's because the bond you're holding may have been locked in at a lower yielding rate than market value, but at any coupon rate, interest rates rise and the price you can sell your bonds for goes down (it's a long topic to dissect). Conversely if interest rates fall, your bond price will rise. With any investment, it is all about timing for buy and sell. Interest rates and having an understanding of their current & future potential for falling or rising will have an impact on all investment options available to you in the marketplace.

- *Cash flow*—I have a friend with a decent amount of cash sitting in a bank. For him, a $10,000 cash purchase on a car didn't dent his cash flow or his ability to pay current and future bills one bit. For some of us, putting a $1,000 down payment on a car cripples cash flow. Know what your monthly bills are (fixed and variable), and analyze how a purchase will impact cash flow on a monthly basis. Line this budget up with the timeframe of the loan versus a one-time hit.

- *Total interest paid*—In certain situations, using a low-interest rate and financing makes sense. At times, you won't pay much in interest (depending on the terms of the loan) and could earn a return on the cash you kept in pocket by financing. Maybe Mr. Smart Guy paying $10,000 cash for a car could have been better off financing the car at a low-interest rate. If he put money to work and earned a higher interest rate on investments than the total interest amount paid on the car, it might have made more sense. Don't assume an all-cash payment is always the best solution. Every financial decision requires proper analysis.

- *Entire financial picture*—This topic is a subset of cash flow. How much cash you have and are able to earn interest on versus how much your monthly spending costs in interest (via credit card debt) is an omnipresent issue. Don't feel bad—the average American household has thousands of dollars in credit card debt. You are not alone. However, if you have debt of any sort, pay down the highest interest debt first. "Hey, I have a few thousand dollars in cash that

I'll put toward buying a new car" may not be the best decision for every buyer in the marketplace. If your car loan is 2 to 3 percent, but you're paying 20 percent interest on your credit card debt, take that cash and pay down your highest interest debt as soon as possible. Identify all pieces of your financial situation and put together scenarios. That way, you can come up with the best plan. If you are unable to do this, hit me up, and I'll charge you a low hourly rate.

- *Opportunity cost of transaction*—This tenet is similar to the previous bullet point. What should you do with your money? Pay down high-interest credit card debt with the cash you're about to use for a purchase? Put money into a high-yield savings account and watch it grow? Waste the cash anyway? Pull the trigger now? Always consider alternative options for your cash, especially with interest rates in mind. Analyze savings and earning a return. On the flip side, analyze debt and paying interest on your purchases.

- *Salvage (resale) value if shit hits the fan*—The technical finance term for how much you can sell an item that sits on your financials (as an asset) is salvage value. Don't worry about accounting transactions personally, but be concerned with the value of any asset purchased and how it devalues over time. Any experienced bum can tell you buying a brand-new car is usually a poor financial decision. Why? Because the second you drive that car off the lot, its value depletes drastically. Furthermore, if you have a loan on that car with no gap insurance (insurance that will cover how much you owe on the car instead of its market value), a crash results in a big personal payout. Insurance will cut you a check for the fair-market car value, but you'll get stuck paying the remaining loan balance. This means you owe more on the loan than the car's market value. Expect to pay the difference out of pocket. For example, *you financed a "Stabbin' Wagon" used Jet Stream for $15,000* *and drove that baby off the lot looking for some fun. A couple of years down the road, you get in a severe car accident, racing through the city, trolling for a Craigslist casual encounter. The "Stabbin' Wagon" is completely totaled, meaning it would cost more to fix it than Kelley Blue Book's estimated value. On top of that, you owe more against the loan than Kelley Blue Book's estimated value.* Let's break it down:

- Amount owed on loan: $13,500
- Salvage Value: $9,500
- Insurance Pays You: $9,500
- Amount owed to bank: $4,000 (if no gap insurance to cover full loan amount)

Kindly see above. With no gap *insurance (to cover the difference between what the car is worth and how much you owe to the bank on loan)*, you would be stuck paying $4,000 out of pocket. Note to self, don't crash a car when repair costs are more than salvage value. Always be thinking about the difference between your car's value and how much you owe on the loan. Research what cars hold their value over time. This is part of good financial decision making.

- *Value of asset at any given time*—The big news after another 2017 Patriots Super Bowl—time will tell how, and if, they cheated vs. the Falcons—was that Tom Brady's Super Bowl jersey went missing. Yeah, this is news, but not news that is going to change my life in any way, shape, or form. "Police say Tom Brady's Super Bowl jersey is worth this much" was the headline. Out of curiosity, I wanted to see what the cops had to say. The Houston police estimated his jersey to be valued at half a million dollars ($500,000). That's a lot of zeros for a jersey that probably cost ten dollars to make. Any asset is only worth as much as you can sell it for (at any given time).

  I once had a boat. A boat is one of the most difficult things to sell. Don't buy a boat. You may think you own a three-thousand-dollar asset because that's what you bought it for. You can't sell that damn thing for one thousand dollars. Any good financial decision should be made with the ability and effort required to sell at the forefront of your mind in the event one desperately needs cash. In other words, I wouldn't pay five hundred dollars for Tom Brady's Super Bowl jersey, let alone five hundred thousand. Maybe someone out there would, maybe not.

If you've ever watched pawn shop shows, people come to collectors with something they believe is priceless. Think of those same people and how sad their faces look when they find a collector would only pay a fraction of the price they expected. Don't be that guy or gal with a sad, moping face when you find out you are "upside down" on your purchase. You owe more on the loan than you'd ever be able to sell for—accept fate.

- *Hold onto any asset until equity*—The onus is on you to play your investment in an asset properly. During the financial crisis of 2008, a big issue was people across the country being upside down on home loans, owing more than their home's value. Douchers took out home equity lines of credit against equity they had in their homes without any intention to sell. This means they essentially threw away any equity in their home to access cash. When the market dipped, these same morons cried wolf like the government owed them something for making bad financial decisions.

  Taxpayers were expected to pay their mortgage plus a line of credit, with interest on both. A wise financial man would never take a line of credit against the equity they have on their home unless they intend to sell that house for more than what they owe on the line of credit taken against the house. In addition, a sage investor would only have a mortgage amount that is manageable. Adding a line of credit increases one's payment amount on the mortgage. Unable to make the mortgage payment plus the payment

> amount of your line of credit? You're a dumbass. You made a bad decision. Don't blame anyone else. Don't crawl on your knees to the government asking for help. You know what you got yourself into.

Any financial investment is a complex decision. Most people don't put thought into interest rates, the future view on interest rates, savings, opportunity cost, cash flow, timing of a buy or sell, salvage value, depreciation, or any other necessary variables required to make a sagacious financial investment. When irresponsible actors blow it and overextend themselves into a hole of debt, that's fine. The issue arises when they want to blame someone else and taxpayers must fund mistakes. Everyone has a sob story (the media loves to use for government control). Let people fail and take personal responsibility. I'd rather rebound, as a taxpayer, than pay for every failure.

Chapter 9

LEVERAGING DEBT

THIS CHAPTER UNLOCKS SECRETS OF FINANCING THAT, if misused, can leave you in a financial wormhole. Read this chapter as a precautionary tale. These financial tools assist in the purchase of necessities that one could not acquire without them. But if you get in over your head, these financial tools can, conversely, cripple you into bankruptcy. Let's start with the (mostly true) proclamation: corporations leverage debt to expand growth. Debt is a necessary tool. Say a company wants to expand regionally, invest in new assets, or needs a new fleet of vehicles to grow revenue or win a large contract—debt is a common tool that allows for that. Maybe more Monica Lewinsky–type sales hookers are required to blowjob their way into new contracts; debt allows for new hires. Maybe the CEO requires more office whores to stroke him under the desk for a cigar-ending climax à la Bill Clinton; debt can get them that.

The first tool required to leverage debt is that one must establish credit. How do you do this as a pimple-faced college kid with freshly sprouted pubic hair and a chocolate milk mustache? Start with a baseline. In statistical and analytical terms, a baseline is a starting point to measure against thereafter. In terms of credit score, kids exit college with jackshit to show for it, aside from student loan debt. To get started, a "secured" credit card is the way to go. Essentially, you put three hundred dollars into an account, pay your bills with that card, and pay it back to a three-hundred-dollar ending cash balance each billing cycle. Simultaneously, sign up with one of the companies that monitors and tracks your credit score. That will provide visibility to all open accounts with statuses. It will also save you from potentially fraudulent accounts that someone may have opened using your Social Security number under your name.

Storytime! The year was 2006. I was fresh out of Claremont Colleges, embarking on a career as an analyst. I landed a salaried job and accepted, foregoing a move to Australia, which was the original plan. I moved to somewhere in Nevada, where there wasn't much for elegance at the time other than big Nevada hair, brothels, and Lake Tahoe for snowboarding. I had a neighbor I dubbed "Hungry Butt" because her ass was so big, it devoured any pair of pants that barely enveloped her sumo-sized physique. I have zero qualms about bad-mouthing this woman, as we ended up in a court case over my conduct as her neighbor. My offenses? Shooting guns, wearing cowboy boots in my underwear, and generally being a modern-day John Wayne type figure—all things that were totally acceptable in 2006 Nevada.

There I was somewhere in Nevada, living next to Hungry Butt and becoming a career man, living that American Dream. Ten minutes down the road was the world-famous Bunny Ranch. I was spending my non-state-taxed paychecks mostly at the bars, buying cigarettes, and snowboarding Tahoe's pristine mountains. Real classy, I know. I was a frequent visitor of the Bunny Ranch as a bar patron, not a John Doe looking for real action in the whores' dorm rooms. The madam became quite annoyed with me and my friends on more than one occasion. We would go there, drink to inebriation while referring to the girls as whores, not their proper term even at that time. "Working girls" is what they were expected to be called. If you have ever been to a brothel, they expect you to be there for sex, not drinks at the bar—even if you throw down a case. You are expected to pick a girl and ask if they will take you on a tour of their dorm room. They then expect you to negotiate a fair price for sex. This can be quite low if you're young and strapping. Old geezers pay a hefty price for those two minutes of glory.

The best part of the Bunny Ranch is getting buzzed in to enter through a domineering white security gate. You pass through the corridor, enter the fine establishment, and the madam calls the girls to line up in unison and announce themselves: "I'm Vanilla, I'm Jasmine, I'm Kimia, I'm Naz, I'm Meagz, I'm Pearlita, I'm Val/Valery (maybe), I'm Jo-Jo (Binx), I'm Debbie Non-Dallas," etc. These "working girls" were engaging in the oldest business transaction known to man—prostitution. Most were operating in a town where nobody knew their names or faces. These girls traveled to the Bunny Ranch from the Midwest (places like Michigan) to fly out for a fortnight, earn their cash, then fly home to boyfriends or whatever else was back in no man's land.

Point being is that I was beginning my career and needed to establish credit. My parents decided to trade in the Chevy Blazer I drove all through college, since I now had a career. I desperately needed to purchase a vehicle. I had yet to establish credit and could only afford an all-wheel drive Subaru for $1,200. While it helped me thrash my way through somewhere in Nevada, mob Lake Tahoe boarding, and avoid cops in blizzards, it was not a long-term solution. Upon this realization, I decided that if I ever wanted to purchase a reliable car, I'd need credit. At that point, no bank was willing to lend me money without a history of paying off my debts.

I got a secured credit card and paid it off every month in full. Within months, Wells Fargo notified me that my credit card was no longer secured and I had a $500 true credit limit, then a $1,500 limit, and then a few years later, my credit card had a $14,000 limit. Again, this was all based on payment history, credit score, and income. During this early period in my financial career, I also decided it was time to start monitoring my credit score. This would help determine when, with a good credit score, I would be eligible for low-interest rates to purchase a car to drop panties at somewhere besides the local Cactus Club Casino.

I signed up for one of the many services that offer visibility into all three major credit scoring companies. They track credit usage, open accounts, and rate you with a numeric score. Currently, I pay the annual $35 fee for one of those that gives you active email alerts and a monthly analysis as anything changes. And here is why: when I checked my credit report for the first time, I had a few accounts with payments past due. One was a gas credit card account and another credit card. Both were showing delinquent. For the sake of taking the higher road, I will not address this person here in this book, as it has been handled in person mano a mano. But someone close to me had taken out credit cards using my Social Security number and information while I was in high school and then didn't pay the cards off.

If someone has access to your Social Security number, it is very easy for them to exploit you, from a financial standpoint. If you're the dumbass who thinks, "Oh, I live in a cash world," then you are stuck centuries behind because some crook-face out there would love to have access to your credit and debt leveraging capabilities. The outcome of this story is that I contested the delinquencies to all three of the major credit agencies. I wrote statements that the activity was fraudulent, as it was, and had them both removed from my credit report. I also made it clear that if an investigation popped up, I would tell the whole truth about who had tampered with my Social Security number and opened accounts in my name without my knowledge or consent. Not the best start to establishing a credit rapport, but at least I found out sooner rather than later. This could have gone on for years had I lived in the "cash only" mindset or failed to dig into my credit history.

Not that the "cash only" mindset is wrong. I have some extremely shrewd compatriots who would argue the cash-gold mindset is the only realm in which one should be investing or indulging. However, if I had maintained that mindset, I'd still be driving a $1,500 Subaru wagon that started costing me more in repairs than the car was even worth. The reason I make this point is that debt financing is essential for certain scenarios as long as it doesn't impact your ability to maintain positive cash flow and pay your bills. And for people who do not have a head start in life, like family money that allows them to pay for a $30,000 car all cash, when starting one's career, financing a car purchase is necessary. I would argue that financing a car beats paying all cash, even if you do have a large chunk of $30,000 in the bank. This is due to time value of money principles and contingent upon interest rate environment for borrowing & savings.

In comes credit, and with it comes danger. Danger, Will Robinson, danger! But it also brings the potential to purchase assets that will hold their value and that you can resell and upgrade at a certain point. Let's put it this way: debt is a slippery slope. It can be like the Asian massage parlor that gives happy endings and becomes addicting. Once a person discovers the simple sin of getting a handjob with oil, followed by a hot towel and alcohol rubdown, they think, "No big deal." And let's face it, a good old-fashioned hand job here and there in sanitary conditions is no big deal. But what happens when you start making that a morning routine? What happens when the handjob no longer suffices, and you expose your genitals to oral sex and eventually start heading to plow-town? Pretty soon, you have an addiction problem and possibly a debt problem to go along with it, as these AMPs are no longer the $60 drop-in-and-drop-out locations they were back in the early 2000s. Not that I would know, but I've heard through men who are less risk-averse than myself. I repeat, Asian massage parlors that give happy endings and debt financing are both slippery, addicting slopes. Enter each with caution.

Before engaging in any debt venture, one must have a monthly cash flow budget. That means you must know how much cash comes in from all income sources and how much goes out on all expenses. From there, you can determine a positive cash flow and total amount. We've already established that one must begin their credit history with a secured card. The next step is to get a credit card with a line of credit limit. And the ultimate goal is that you should pay it off entirely at the end of each statement. Now, let me repeat myself: pay off all that you spend at the end of each monthly statement. So if you have that $14,000 line of credit on your card, it doesn't mean keep your credit card at a $10,000 balance, because that 25 percent interest adds up. It can be an additional few hundred dollars monthly that you must pay back.

Credit card interest rates are a real burden for a few reasons. The spread between interest rates that banks lend cash to large corporations or other banks has widened from that which banks can lend to individual customers. For individual consumer credit card interest rates, the spread is excessive. You may as well open wide and expect to get hit with a 12-inch finance charge every month if you are carrying a large amount of credit card debt. While debt financing can help you, in the form of credit card debt, it will likely cripple you. The one exception I have leveraged for debt financing is "Care Credit," which is zero-percent financing for medical or sometimes other health-related items that offer zero-percent financing if paid back within the allotted time frame. I also found the ability to leverage it on specific home appliance purchases. But if you don't pay back on time, the usual high-interest rates apply.

Another key thing to monitor is your entire financial picture, knowing where your high-interest debt resides. Which credit card has high-interest rates, like that one girl you took home from the dive bar and still lives with you today? Rearrange or move your debt. If you are paying a credit card that carries a $5,000 balance, you may be getting hit with high finance charges monthly. In some cases, you can move that debt to a credit card that offers zero-percent interest for balance transfers for your first eighteen months. Other tactics to save on paying interest include getting a loan through your credit union or bank that offers a fixed, low-interest rate so you know exactly what your monthly payment will be (principal plus fixed interest). It will almost always be lower than the variable and exorbitantly high credit card rates currently prevalent in most of the market.

If you are a homeowner, the temptation is always there to take a home equity line to pay off your outstanding, high-interest credit card debts. Let's not forget that one culprit for the financial collapse of 2008 was that many homeowners thought they were wealthy, taking out home equity loans and lines of credit. Let's be frank: if you take out a loan against your house, you are, for the most part, making a poor decision. This is just my personal opinion, and there are situations where it may make sense. For example, if you have a ton of equity in your house & plan to sell in the next few years, you can sell with enough profit to pay off that loan, make money on the sale, and purchase somewhere else that is a better-value home purchase.

Always upgrade wisely. Another example would be taking out a home equity loan to upgrade your house, for something to make it more valuable on the market or to you personally. But just remember, you have to pay the debt back and your monthly payment rises. But in general, home equity loans and lines of credit are for those who lack better financial planning, especially if they never intend to sell their home or turn it into income.

However, most people who take loans against their homes have no future plan to sell their home, pay back that loan, earn a profit on the sale, and then purchase another home for a better value. So, basically, they take a loan out against their home. Great job, shit brick. Let's discuss the pitfalls of that home equity loan. A loan is a loan and must be paid back. When you take out a home equity loan, it must still be paid back. And when you use your home as collateral for the loan, that means if you don't pay the loan back, the bank can come in and take ownership (full or partial) of your home. If that white trash, *Eastbound & Down* ten-thousand-dollar Jet Ski was really worth losing your home over, then so be it. But let's not act like the uneducated, boats-and-hoes-first kind of homeowner and make these mistakes.

Here's another secret about real estate. I learned this from my first job after college, working for a production homebuilder in Nevada. While your wife (or maybe softy husband) gets their panties juicy walking through a new home, take a step back and say, "Fuck the house!" Ask yourself what it is you are actually paying for. In Nevada, nice-looking production homes in a brand-new development are fun to walk through. You may think it's a wise decision to get into a new development with cheesedick appliances and a faux-silver microwave.

Truth be told, in desert areas like Nevada, you can build those homes into oblivion, and their value will never appreciate relative to the market of truly unique and scarce real estate. Now, if you want to retire there with an affordable monthly mortgage, that's a different story. But don't think for a second that as the population in that state grows, they can't build brand-new production houses into the desert until blue in the balls. Your place will continue to grow older as new neighborhoods pop up, making yours less desirable. It's the desert; the land is consistently barren. This brings us to the juice of the matter.

You don't invest in homes. New homes can be built poorly, cheaply, and in the shittiest of geographies forever and ever. If you want to invest in a home, it needs to be a place that cannot be easily replicated. It needs to have the characteristics of a stable economy, good weather, low crime rates, beaches or mountains, nice parks, clean air and water, outdoor recreation activities, highly-rated schools, and other defining criteria that are not readily available in every city, state, or nation. You purchase land, location, and quality of life. If any of the above are garbage, the investment in a new home is garbage. Don't be suckered into the idea of a new home if the development is in tweaker land and you'll have to fight zombies off your property every night.

What factors keep a place desirable to live? Pittsburgh used to be a huge steel-mining town. That industry went dead, and the town turned morbid. There are countless abandoned gold and silver mining towns left over from the gold rush. While we have a modern economy and there are certain black swan events that are unforeseen, certain areas have unique characteristics that will always make them desirable—unless government destroys them with socialism.

Obviously, other industries have taken over the modern economy, and times change, but the line of reasoning still needs to be at the forefront of your mind when investing in real estate. I own a place in a small beach community in California, one of the most expensive real estate markets in the world. Now, there is no way in hell I would have purchased one of those overpriced three-bedroom, two-bath, million-dollar plus fix-me-uppers in the quaint beach community where I reside. Instead, I found a two-bedroom, one-bath condo at the back end of a neighborhood, with gorgeous mountain views. I paid three hundred eighty-nine thousand dollars (in 2016), which was unheard of for this area, even at that time. The reason I was able to get in at that price is because my condo is located in a neighborhood that is a bit congested, with most other condos having views of a similar-looking building across from it. When I say congested, compared to LA, this beach community neighborhood is the land of the free and super safe. I bought at the far back of the neighborhood, with a private entrance road and clear mountain views that are breathtaking every day of the year. Without an eye for real estate, this place was priced the same as other condos in the same area with no mountain views. I tell people I have a million-dollar view because I do. And the neighborhood has only appreciated substantially across the board because of all the other factors that have made this city a great place for long-term investment.

I'm not saying this to boast but to drive home the point: you do not simply invest or buy a house! The decision is complex, and you pay for location and land. Are you in the year-round summer of California with mountain views and walking distance to the beach? Or are you in buttfuck-Timbuktu, Nevada, where you could walk and develop that worthless desert land for the next one hundred years in the same fashion? Supply and demand, my friends.

To be thorough on the largest debt investment of your life, the first thought should be that you are willing to stay in that place for thirty years and pay back the mortgage in its entirety. If a situation arises where you have a great amount of equity and want to upgrade, reanalyze your situation then. For now, can you manage the mortgage payments for thirty years? What if a black swan event hits the economy and impacts your family directly? A black swan event is when the most unforeseen, unexpected financial collapse happens to you personally or to financial markets. The term is more commonly used for disasters such as the Great Depression or the Great Recession of 2008. But it also needs to be in the back of your mind when you invest in a home. Always think about the worst-case scenario and how you would react. What happens if there is a real estate crash in your area? Would the circumstances still be the same, or would you be stuck renting out your place for eight hundred dollars with a two-thousand-dollar monthly mortgage payment? These thoughts need to be analyzed carefully before taking out four hundred thousand dollars in debt. At the end of the day, purchasing a home is a debt investment. It's one that can provide substantial gain or tragic loss.

But if your priorities are a Jet Ski and a mullet, Kenny Powers could give you some great investing tips. You may even end up making a comeback as a used car salesman. But who cares? As long as you have a chick with big old '80s hair in a leotard on the back in Oakley blades, that Jet Ski is priceless. Take out that home equity loan and a line of credit. Milk it until the bank comes in and repos your home. Be a bastardo or not.

Chapter 10

CLOSING

If you are still reading this, I want to congratulate you for not being a total pussy. You have officially become a *B-School Bastardo.* I hope you have found value and are the type of person this society needs. I appreciate your support and curiosity. It is rather sad we have entered into a period of American history where there is a palpable war occurring daily against free speech. From my stance, I don't give a shit what someone says. If I disagree, I will avoid listening to their opinion entirely. Many in charge of powerful societal systems and large aspects of government and media want all opinions disavowed and disallowed they do not agree with. I say fuck that.

Thank you for reading. I wrote this book—*mostly*—when I was fresh out of business school, having attained my MBA with a finance concentration. I had the idea to write a book using a lot of satire and perverse humor on complex topics, giving real-world examples from life experiences. A lot of the topics I selected were things I wish I had known when I was a young grom. My intent was to cater to an audience with a lack of experience or parental assistance in the real world. This book is for the underdogs and people who have not been born on third base and acted like they hit that triple. I wrote this book to myself at a younger age. I have always loved writing. My intent had always been to write non-fiction under the guise of fiction. But I wanted to write a technical book first because it would be the most difficult. And it will likely be rejected by the audience I'm asking to publish it for the mainstream population. I do know if this book hits the right listeners, it will be meaningful. I'm not one who is big for goodbyes. Hence, you can see there is no major closing chapter or prologue. I wrote the chapters. I did not add any fluff. I pulled the Irish goodbye. Until the next one, all my best!

About the Author

J. Bo Lawrence's inspiration for writing was initially (and simply) using a silver tongue to make humor of life's unusual situations. While his career spanned finance, data analytics, operations, inventory, purchasing, mid- to senior-level management, FP&A, and CFO level, he considers himself a small-town kid, always. J. Bo Lawrence has been published in local news, both as an undercover journalist and a visible voice during local hot topics. The majority of his first book was written fresh out of business school, having graduated Beta Gamma Sigma honors from Pepperdine's Graziadio School of Business and Management with an MBA in finance, while working a full-time corporate job. He also holds an undergraduate degree from the renowned Claremont Colleges (*International Relations, History*). While he always felt like an outcast during academia and professional life (having attended public schools), he is comfortably at home as a lover and a fighter. His true passions lie in the martial arts and water worlds. J. Bo Lawrence holds a second-degree black belt in Brazilian jiujitsu and is a multiple-time national and world champion medalist. He also is an avid surfer, fisher, barbecuer, and snowboarder. Yet, his biggest passions are friends, family, and animals.

www.ingramcontent.com/pod-product-compliance
Lightning Source LLC
LaVergne TN
LVHW090406210926
848480LV00002B/475
* 9 7 9 8 8 9 6 1 7 3 8 5 4 *